THE COMMUNITY INTEF

EXERCISES AND ROLE PLAYS

A Companion Workbook for

THE COMMUNITY INTERPRETER
A Comprehensive Training Manual (5th ed, 2011)

Marjory A. Bancroft, MA, and Lourdes Rubio-Fitzpatrick, MA, LPC

This workbook of exercises supports
THE COMMUNITY INTERPRETER
A Comprehensive Training Manual (5th ed, 2011)

Culture and Language Press

A Division of

Cross-Cultural Communications
10015 Old Columbia Road, Suite B-215
Columbia, MD 21046
Voice: 410-312-5599
Fax: 410-750-0332
ccc@cultureandlanguage.net
www.cultureandlanguage.net

TABLE OF CONTENTS

PROGRAM GOAL AND OBJECTIVES

LEARNING OBJECTIVES

*Upon completing THE COMMUNITY INTERPRETER,
a 40-hour certificate program, participants will be
able to:*

UNIT 1   ETHICS AND CONDUCT (8 hours)

Objective 1.1
Demonstrate knowledge about the profession of community interpreting.
> 1.1 (a) Discuss the history of community interpreting.
> 1.1 (b) List the qualifications and skills of community interpreters.
> 1.1 (c) Address the impact of language access laws on community interpreting.
> 1.1 (d) Develop awareness of self-monitoring and self-assessment for interpreters.

Objective 1.2
Apply ethical principles for interpreters to simulated situations from real life.
> 1.2 (a) Describe the differences between ethics and standards of practice.
> 1.2 (b) Discuss ethics and standards for community interpreters.
> 1.2 (c) Develop strategies to apply ethical principles in real-life settings.

UNIT 2   INTERPRETER SKILLS (8 hours)

Objective 2.1
Execute an interpreted session.
> 2.1 (a) List the steps to execute an interpreted session.
> 2.1 (b) Discuss and select appropriate modes of interpreting.
> 2.1 (c) Practice interpreting in consecutive and simultaneous modes.
> 2.1 (d) Demonstrate basic sight translation skills.

Objective 2.2
Analyze and practice basic interpreter skills.
> 2.2 (a) Demonstrate professional introductions, positioning and use of direct speech.
> 2.2 (b) Develop message analysis, note-taking and memory skills sufficient to
>   interpret two to three sentences accurately without asking for repetition.
> 2.2 (c) Practice basic interpreting skills in simple role plays.

UNIT 3   CULTURE AND MEDIATION (8 hours)

Objective 3.1
Demonstrate effective mediation skills.
>   3.1 (a) List and practice the steps for mediation.
>   3.1 (b) Practice strategic mediation.
>   3.1 (c) Define and compare interpreter roles.

Objective 3.2
Develop and practice cultural mediation strategies.
>   3.2 (a) Define culture and cultural competence.
>   3.2 (b) Apply ethical decision-making to a communication barrier.
>   3.2 (c) Practice non-intrusive cultural mediation.
>   3.2 (d) Show awareness of stereotypes and bias.

UNIT 4   COMMUNITY SERVICES (4 hours)

Objective 4
Develop skill sets in specific sectors of community interpreting.
>   4.1 Contrast and compare legal and community interpreting.
>   4.2 Discuss service systems in healthcare, education and/or human and social services and their impact on interpreters.
>   4.3 Develop strategies to enhance competence in terminology.

UNIT 5   STANDARDS OF PRACTICE (10 hours)

Objective 5.1
Develop a working knowledge of national standards of practice.
>   5.1 (a) Review the 32 NCIHC national standards of practice.
>   5.1 (b) Discuss strategies for promoting and practicing standards.
>   5.1 (c) Act out standards of practice in challenging situations from real life.

Objective 5.2
Apply national standards of practice to interpreting.
>   5.2 (a) Demonstrate the application of standards of practice in community service settings.
>   5.2 (b) Relate ethics and standards to professional development for interpreters.

Introduction

This workbook supports the 5th edition of *THE COMMUNITY INTERPRETER: A Comprehensive Training Manual*. That manual in turn supports a certificate program in community interpreting. Both *THE COMMUNITY INTERPRETER* and this workbook are used to present a 40- to 60-hour program in general community interpreting and/or specialized sectors of community interpreting, such as healthcare or education.

Instructors who purchase a copy of this workbook may find the exercises useful but should not call this program *THE COMMUNITY INTERPRETER* unless they have also attended the Training-of-Trainers program delivered by Cross-Cultural Communications and signed a licensing agreement to present *THE COMMUNITY INTERPRETER*. Trainers should also note that it is a violation of U.S. and international copyright law to photocopy substantial portions of any book. (A few pages may be photocopied for educational purposes.)

Many of the activities in this workbook apply to three major sectors of community interpreting: health care; education; and human and social services. Other activities are specific to one sector, such as healthcare; these sector-specific activities are clearly labeled so that the instructor can make an informed decision about which activities to select for a particular group. Thus, if you are an instructor who works solely with healthcare interpreters, you may select the role plays and skills-building activities that pertain only to healthcare interpreting. If you are an interpreter who wants to practice your skills (e.g. by self recording the role plays in this book or studying the manual and following the workbook activities) you, too, can focus on one particular sector or on all sectors of community interpreting.

The exercises and activities in this workbook are intended only as a guide. Each instructor will select those that seem most suitable for a particular program or group. Licensed trainers for this program will also select the particular exercises in this workbook that best meet the needs of the group. They are authorized to substitute any exercises in this workbook with their own activities and exercises provided that all learning objectives are adequately addressed.

For information on Training-of-Trainer sessions for *THE COMMUNITY INTERPRETER,* please call 410-312-5599 or contact ccc@cultureandlanguage.net.

How to Use This Workbook

This workbook follows the general structure of THE COMMUNITY INTERPRETER. Its activities support the objectives of the program and are divided into the same units (Units 1 through 5).

Activities in this workbook fall into four broad categories:
1. Role plays
2. Skills building (practice exercises)
3. Case studies
4. General small-group activities

The role plays and skills-building exercises fall into three core sectors of community interpreting:
1. Healthcare interpreting
2. Educational interpreting (e.g., K-12 schools, Head Start, community colleges)
3. Human and social services

However, this workbook contains too many exercises to be used during a 40-hour program. Most of the exercises are designed for use in classroom settings and a number can be used to support a longer program of 60 hours, which allows more time for skills-building, practice and exercises. Many exercises are labeled by sector so that instructors may focus on one sector of community services by selecting role plays and skills-building activities from that sector alone, such as health care. Many activities are relevant to all sectors.

A number of the exercises, especially the optional activities, may be given as home assignments and discussed in class or used for in-services and continuing education programs. Still others may be used at the instructor's discretion for more advanced groups.

Finally, for groups that want or need additional practice, an appendix includes supplementary role plays that can be selected at the trainer's discretion to address the needs of a particular group or a particular sub-sector of community interpreting at any relevant point in the program.

ABOUT THE AUTHORS

Marjory Bancroft, MA

Marjory Bancroft is a national leader in the development of training programs for community interpreting, cultural competence and language access and has over 30 years in the field of language and education. She holds a BA and MA in French linguistics from Quebec City in addition to advanced language certificates from Spain, Germany, and Jordan. After an early career teaching translation, English and French for two universities, two immigrant schools in Montreal, continuing education programs and the Canadian Embassy in Washington DC, she spent several years interpreting, translating and directing an immigrant health program and a language bank of 200 interpreters and translators.

A past Board member of the National Council on Interpreting in Healthcare, Marjory now sits on the Board of Advocates for Survivors of Torture and Trauma, the Advisory Committee for the NCIHC national healthcare interpreter training standards, the ISO subcommittee to establish international standards for community interpreting, and the interpreting subcommittee of ASTM International. She is also the Executive Director of THE VOICE OF LOVE, a national, all-volunteer project devoted to guiding those who interpret for survivors of torture, trauma and sexual violence. The author of numerous training manuals, facilitator guides and workbooks on community and healthcare interpreting and four train-the-instructor manuals for cultural competence, she speaks widely at conferences across the U.S.

Lourdes Rubio-Fitzpatrick, MA, L.P.C., D.A.P.A.

Lourdes immigrated to the U.S. from Mexico City. A practicing interpreter and bilingual counselor with Arlington Public Schools in Virginia, she has more than 25 years of experience in the field of conference, community, legal, government and educational interpreting. Lourdes is fluent in Spanish, English, French, American Sign Language and Mexican Sign Language. She holds an MA in Special Education and an MA in Counseling from Gallaudet University. She is a lecturer on community and educational interpreting and translation for George Mason University. She is also an experienced instructor for healthcare, legal and community interpreters.

In addition to co-authoring THE COMMUNITY INTERPRETER, Lourdes authored another training manual, *An Introduction to Community Interpreting* (published by Northern Virginia Area Health Education Center). Lourdes' many translations include *A Basic Course in Sign Language.* In addition to developing several interpreting training curricula and programs for those who work with interpreters, she has contributed to the development of a computer program, *Mexican Sign Language/ American Sign Language Translator (*by the Institute for Disabilities Research and Training). Previously, Lourdes worked as a therapist and contributed to teen pregnancy and drug abuse prevention programs for Latinos in Washington, D.C. A licensed counselor, she supported the development of counseling services and parenting classes for Latino families in Virginia and has helped to create the office of Hispanic Services at Gallaudet University. Lourdes is also one of the principal curriculum authors for THE VOICE OF LOVE, a national, nonprofit project devoted to guiding those who interpret for survivors of torture, trauma and sexual violence, and she is a member of their Board.

UNIT 1   ETHICS AND CONDUCT

OBJECTIVE 1.1
Demonstrate knowledge about the profession of community interpreting.

1.1 (a) Discuss the history of community interpreting.
1.1 (b) List the qualifications and skills of community interpreters.
1.1 (c) Address the impact of language access laws on community interpreting.
1.1 (d) Develop awareness of self-monitoring and self-assessment for interpreters.

Exercise 1-a   Community Interpreting

In pairs, *without looking at your textbook,* answer the following questions:

1. What does an interpreter do? _____

_____

_____

2. Name some common sectors of interpreting (e.g., conference interpreting).

_____

_____

_____

_____

3. What is community interpreting?

_____

_____

_____

4. What do you know about the history of community interpreting?

_____

_____

_____

Exercise 1-b   Qualifications and Skills

Working in pairs or groups of three, describe the <u>minimum</u> set of qualifications and skills that you think a community interpreter should demonstrate before being allowed to interpret professionally:

Qualifications (e.g., level of education)

_____

_____

_____

Skills (e.g., able to interpret 2-3 sentences accurately)

_____
_____
_____

Now list any other qualifications and skills you think are <u>desirable</u> for community interpreters to have:

_____
_____
_____

Exercise 1-c   **Certification**

What types of organizations develop professional certification? (Consider certification for any profession, not only for interpreting.)

_____
_____
_____

Give examples of specific organizations that have developed certification for interpreters.

_____
_____
_____

Give examples (if any) of certification programs that have been developed in the U.S. or in your own country for:

Court interpreting

_____
_____

Sign language interpreting

_____
_____

Community interpreting

_____
_____

Healthcare interpreting (note: healthcare interpreting is part of community interpreting, but because it is the most professionalized sector of community interpreting, it has developed specialized certification in the U.S.)

_____
_____

Exercise 1-d   **Role Plays**

The following two role plays are for two people. Simply read them out loud. These are English-language role plays, so you do not need to speak the same language.

After each pair completes the first role play, switch roles so that both of you play the interpreter. Then go to the second role play and do the same.

1. Qualified Interpreter Role Play

Number of participants: 2
Setting: Job interview for a community-based organization
Roles: Interpreter and potential employer

Employer: Are you a certified interpreter?
Interpreter: No. I am a community interpreter. Outside the state of Washington, there's no certification for community interpreters, only for healthcare interpreters.
Employer: So why should I hire you?
Interpreter: I have a certificate for a 40-hour program of professional training in community interpreting, and I have been tested for language proficiency in my working languages. I'm considered a *qualified interpreter.*

2. Certified Interpreter Role Play

Number of participants: 2
Setting: Job interview for a healthcare organization
Roles: Interpreter and potential employer

Employer: Are you a certified interpreter?
Interpreter: Yes. I was recently certified by CCHI.
Employer: What's that?
Interpreter: Certification Commission for Healthcare Interpreters. Here's my documentation.
Employer: Wait. Didn't I hear about another national certification?
Interpreter: Yes, NBCMI—the National Board of Certification for Medical Interpreters.
Employer: Okay. That's what I thought. Is this one better than the other one?
Interpreter: The two exams are a bit different, but they're both accepted in the field as professional certification.

Exercise 1-e   **Oral Self-assessment**

Where possible, work in *same-language* pairs for this exercise. Take turns playing the interpreter. Also, any non-Spanish interpreter who plays the patient (Text A) or parent (Text B) should try to *sight translate the patient/parent text into the target language.*

Note: It is advisable, after hearing the instructions, to *watch a demonstration* of two individuals acting out this exercise so that you understand exactly what to do.

Follow these steps:

1. Turn on your recording device to make certain it is working.
2. Partner One will play the Interpreter and *will not look at the text*. Partner Two will read aloud *both the Client (Text A=Patient, Text B=Parent)* <u>and</u> *the Provider (Text A=Doctor, Text B=Assistant Principal)*, using both languages if possible. Leave time after every two sentences for the interpreter to interpret. A Spanish-English script is provided. All other interpreters should use the English script beside the Spanish-English version. (If neither Partner is a Spanish interpreter but both share another language, the person who plays the Patient or Parent will orally translate the Patient/Parent text into the other language, e.g., Russian, to help the Interpreter practice both languages. Read the Provider's text out loud in English.)
3. Partner One: turn on your recording device and ***<u>DO NOT LOOK AT THE TEXT</u>***.
4. Partner Two: Read Text A (healthcare).
5. As Partner Two reads out the lines for the Doctor and the Patient (translating the Patient's lines if needed). Partner One (Interpreter) will perform consecutive interpreting. Record this session.
6. Do not interrupt the session for any reason after you turn on the recording device. Ignore any mistakes. Just keep interpreting until the end of the text.
7. After Text A is finished, both partners should look at the questions below and help the Interpreter write down the answers *in the Interpreter's workbook.*
8. Reverse roles for Text B. Partner One will now read Text B (schools), playing both the Parent and the Assistant Principal. Partner Two will play the Interpreter and **<u>WILL NOT LOOK AT THE TEXT</u>**. Partner Two will interpret everything that is said. Follow the instructions above (1-7).
9. If time remains, after finishing Text B, go back to Text A. Do the same exercise all over again but reverse the roles. This time, Partner Two will play the Interpreter for Text A, and Partner One will play the Interpreter for Text B.
10. Continue recording without interruption (except to give each other feedback) until the instructor announces that it is time to stop recording.

TEXT A **HEALTHCARE: Osteoporosis**

Spanish-English

Patient: Doctor, realmente necesito su ayuda. No sé si hacerme un examen de densidad ósea o no. A lo mejor tengo osteoporosis, ya que mi mamá la tiene.

Doctor: I'd be happy to talk about that. Let's see, you're—66, and you've never had one? Then yes. Usually at your age it's a very good idea to get a bone density test so we can find out if you're at risk for osteoporosis or not.

Patient: ¿Y qué es lo que hace el examen?

Doctor: Basically it tests your bone strength.

Patient: ¿Por qué piensa que debería hacerme el examen?

Doctor: Well, let's say you're at risk for osteoporosis, and the test shows us that. Finding out early if you have it means we can treat it before it gets worse. That could help slow down the rate of bone loss, which would make your bones less likely to break.

Patient: ¿El examen duele? ¿Tarda mucho?

Doctor: Not at all. It's like an X-ray: it just scans your body. It only takes about 15 minutes.

English only

Patient: Doctor, I really need your help. I don't know if I should get a bone density test. Maybe I have osteoporosis, since my mother has it.

Doctor: I'd be happy to talk about that. Let's see, you're—66, and you've never had one? Then yes. Usually at your age it's a very good idea to get a bone density test so we can find out if you're at risk for osteoporosis or not.

Patient: So what does the test do?

Doctor: Basically it tests your bone strength.

Patient: Why do you think I should get the test?

Doctor: Well, let's say you're at risk for osteoporosis, and the test shows us that. Finding out early if you have it means we can treat it before it gets worse. That could help slow down the rate of bone loss, which would make your bones less likely to break.

Patient: Does the test hurt? Is it long?

Doctor: Not at all. It's like an X-ray: it just scans your body. It only takes about 15 minutes.

Patient: Bueno, para ser honesta, tengo un poquito de miedo a los exámenes. ¿Es grave la osteoporosis?

Doctor: It can be, sure. Usually people with osteoporosis break their hip or spine or wrist more often than someone else. And broken bones hurt. They cause a lot of pain and disability, and even daily activities can be hard. So definitely, we want to avoid any broken bones if we can.

Patient: ¿Hay mucha gente con este mal?

Doctor: It's more common than people realize, yes. About 10 million Americans have it, and one of every two women and one in four men over the age of 50 will break a bone at some point in their life because of osteoporosis.

Patient: ¡De verdad, da miedo! Bueno, me voy a hacer el examen. ¿Pero me lo pagará el Medicare?

Doctor: Yes, because you're female and over 65, Medicare will cover it. So let's set you up with an appointment.

Patient: I'm a little scared of tests, to be honest. Is osteoporosis serious?

Doctor: It can be, sure. Usually people with osteoporosis break their hip or spine or wrist more often than someone else. And broken bones hurt. They cause a lot of pain and disability, and even daily activities can be hard. So definitely, we want to avoid any broken bones if we can.

Patient: Do many people have this condition?

Doctor: It's more common than people realize, yes. About 10 million Americans have it, and one of every two women and one in four men over the age of 50 will break a bone at some point in their life because of osteoporosis.

Patient: That sounds scary! Okay, I'm going to have the test. But will Medicare pay for it?

Doctor: Yes, because you're female and over 65, Medicare will cover it. So let's set you up with an appointment.

Text A: Assessment by the partner and the interpreter

Now replay the recording and note down answers in the categories below. Help each other identify the answers. If you are the interpreter's partner and do not speak the interpreter's language, the interpreter will have to perform most of this self assessment alone.

However, <u>even if you do not speak your partner's language</u>, listen carefully and try to give feedback. For example, you could say: *"I noticed in this section your delivery was very confident and smooth. Over here, you had quite a few hesitations, so I wondered if the healthcare terminology was hard for you. Also, this part that you interpreted sounded very short—did you interpret everything I said?"*

Comments on everything the interpreter performed well or smoothly:

_____

_____

Number of times the Interpreter *omitted* something in the text (did not interpret it): _____

Number of times the Interpreter *added* something to the text: _____

Number of times the Interpreter *changed* the text: _____

Number of grammatical errors: _____

Other errors: (specify)

_____

_____

_____

Which parts appeared more difficult to interpret? Why?

_____

_____

Note any other comments or suggestions:

_____

_____

Spanish-English

English only

Assistant Principal (AP): Good morning, Ms. Martinez. My name is John Smith, one of the assistant principals of this school. What can I do for you today?

Parent: Si, mire, vengo echando chispas, por lo que esos gringos le hicieron a mi patojito. Y yo quiero saber qué es lo que usted va a hacer al respecto.

AP: No, I am sorry I don't know what happened to your son, Manuel. Please tell me.

Parent: Vea, ayer después de la escuela mi patojo llegó a la casa llorando y me dijo que dos gringos de esta escuela lo maltrataron y lo golpearon con una pelota en sus cositas en la parada del autobús, y mi patojo pasó toda la noche con dolor. Esta mañana cuando me he despertado sus cositas están bien hinchadas y le duelen mucho.

AP: I am very sorry that this happened to your son. Is Manuel here in school today?

Parent: ¡No! Que no ve que ni siquiera puede caminar. Se quedó en la casa dormido mientras yo vine a quejarme. Porque yo quiero que usted castigue a esos dos niños.

AP: I understand, Ms. Martinez. You have a right to be upset, and I assure you these boys will be punished for what they did. Now, can you please tell me if your son told you the names of these boys?

Assistant Principal (AP): Good morning, Ms. Martinez. My name is John Smith, one of the assistant principals of this school. What can I do for you today?

Parent: Yes, well I am really fuming about what those guys did to my little boy. And I want to know what you are going to do about it.

AP: No, I am sorry I don't know what happened to your son, Manuel. Please tell me.

Parent: Well, yesterday after school my son came home crying and told me that two guys from this school picked on him, and hit him with a ball in his private parts at the bus stop. My son was in pain all night. This morning when I woke up, his private parts were all swollen and they hurt him a lot.

AP: I am very sorry that this happened to your son. Is Manuel here in school today?

Parent: No! He can't even walk. He stayed home sleeping while I came to complain, because I want you to punish those two boys.

AP: I understand, Ms. Martinez. You have a right to be upset, and I assure you that these boys will be punished for what they did. Now, can you please tell me if your son told you the names of these boys?

14

Parent: Sí, aquí los tengo apuntados en este pedazo de papel. Vea usted, yo no sé como pronunciarlos, así que tome el papel.

AP: I want you to know that the school has a strict policy against bullying and fighting. The students are well aware of this policy and know that this type of behavior will not be tolerated.

Parent: Si, pero quiero que sepa que ésta no es la primera vez que pasa. Manuelito, como yo le llamo, me ha dicho que siempre le están haciendo burla porque es gordito y también me le llaman sobrenombres constantemente. Mi patojo ya ni quiere venir a la escuela por eso. Por eso es que yo estoy muy enojada y decidí venir hoy.

AP: Thank you. You did the right thing by coming this morning and letting us know this was happening.

Parent: Ahora, yo necesito llevarlo al doctor para que me lo chequee, pero no tengo seguro y tampoco, estoy trabajando. Dígame usted cómo le hago. Sin dinero ni seguro ningún médico quiere atender a uno. Yo estoy aquí sola, y tampoco tengo marido que me ayude con los gastos. La migra lo deportó hace un año y no ha vuelto.

AP: I understand your concern. Please let me talk to the school nurse and see if she can refer you to a clinic nearby that can see your son right away. Hopefully it will be free of charge or at low cost to you. Would that be okay with you?

Parent: Yes, I have them written down on this piece of paper. Here, I don't know how to pronounce them, so take this paper.

AP: I want you to know that the school has a strict policy against bullying and fighting. The students are well aware of this policy and know that this type of behavior will not be tolerated.

Parent: Yes, but I want you to know that this isn't the first time that this has happened. Manuelito, as I call him, told me that they are always making fun of him because he's chubby, and they're always calling him names. My son doesn't even want to go to school because of this. That's why I'm so angry and I decided to come in today.

AP: Thank you. You did the right thing by coming this morning and letting us know this was happening.

Parent: Now I need to take him to the doctor to be checked out, but I don't have insurance and I'm not working. What am I supposed to do? Without money or insurance no doctor wants to see you. I'm here alone, and I don't have a husband who helps me with expenses. Immigration deported him a year ago and he hasn't come back.

AP: I understand your concern. Please let me talk to the school nurse and see if she can refer you to a clinic nearby that can see your son right away. Hopefully it will be free of charge or at low cost to you. Would that be okay with you?

Parent: Por supuesto, señor, si usted me hace el favor le agradeceré mucho. Quiero asegurarme que mi patojo no tenga nada grave.

AP: Again, I am sorry about what happened to your son, Manuel. I assure you there will be consequences for the boys' behavior. Thank you for coming, and tell your son we hope he gets better soon.

Parent: Of course, sir, I would be very grateful to you if you would do me that favor. I want to be sure that my son isn't seriously hurt.

AP: Again, I am sorry about what happened to your son, Manuel. I assure you there will beconsequences for the boys' behavior. Thank you for coming, and tell your son we hope he gets better soon.

Text B: Assessment by the partner and the interpreter

Now replay the recording and note down answers in the categories below. Help each other identify the answers. If you are the interpreter's partner and do not speak the interpreter's language, the interpreter will have to perform most of this self assessment alone.

However, <u>even if you do not speak your partner's language</u>, listen carefully and try to give general feedback.

Comments on everything the interpreter performed well or smoothly:

_____

_____

Number of times the Interpreter *omitted* something in the text (did not interpret it): _____
Number of times the Interpreter *added* something to the text: _____
Number of times the Interpreter *changed* the text: _____
Number of grammatical errors: _____
Other errors: (specify)

_____

_____

_____

Which parts appeared more difficult to interpret? Why?

_____

_____

Note any other comments or suggestions:

_____

_____

TEXTS A and B: Interpreter self assessment

__This portion will be executed as a home assignment__, not in class.

Take your recorded exercises home after class and listen to each recording carefully, at least twice. Without looking at your partner's answers above, answer the following questions. (You may listen to the recording as often as you wish, stopping and starting as needed.)

Overall, how easy or hard did it feel when you interpreted during this exercise?

_____

_____

Which parts of the text did you find easy to interpret? Why?

_____

_____

Which parts felt difficult? Were they also the parts you interpreted less accurately?

_____

_____

Overall, how would you assess your accuracy and completeness?

_____

_____

Overall, how would you assess your faithfulness to the spirit and meaning of the dialogues?

_____

_____

OBJECTIVE 1.2
Apply ethical principles for interpreters to simulated situations from real life.

1.2 (a) Describe the differences between ethics and standards of practice.
1.2 (b) Discuss ethics and standards for community interpreters.
1.2 (c) Develop strategies to apply ethical principles in real-life settings.

Exercise 1-f   Ethics and Standards of Practice

In pairs, answer the following questions:

1. What is a code of ethics?

_____

_____

_____

2. What are standards of practice?

_____

3. What is the difference between ethics and standards?

Exercise 1-g (optional) **Comparing Codes of Ethics**

The instructor will divide the group into small groups of three or four. At the beginning of the resource section in the training manual for THE COMMUNITY INTERPRETER (5th ed., pp. 366-373), you will find summaries of six sample interpreter codes of ethics. Alternatively, the instructor may provide you with printed copies. These sample codes address:

- Healthcare/healthcare interpreting (NCIHC)
- Community interpreting (CCIO)
- Court/legal interpreting (NAJIT)
- General interpreting (AUSIT)
- Conference interpreting (AIIC)
- Sign language interpreting (RID)

Your group should briefly review the six codes of ethics and identify:

1) Three principles or canons that are roughly the SAME in all six codes of ethics, e.g. "professionalism" (Do not use this example).

2) Three principles or canons that are DIFFERENT: that is, they may be found in *one or two* of the codes of ethics, but not in all six codes. As an example, "professional solidarity," can be found in one code of ethics only. (Do not use this example.)

Exercise 1-h **Mini Case Studies**

The instructor will divide the class into pairs or groups of three. Each group will receive one card with a printed scenario from the list below. Answer the questions on your group's card (take two or three minutes); then answer all the questions you have time for for all the case studies below. The instructor will then ask the whole group to discuss answers for all the situations described below.

The client speaks so rapidly you get lost. Quickly, you try to summarize everything that you can remember about what the client said.

Is summarizing acceptable? Why (or why not)? If not, when is it acceptable to summarize?

_____

_____

Which ethical principles are involved?

_____

The client is so grateful for your wonderful interpreting that she wants to give you a little present: a hand-made doll from her country.

Should you accept? Why (or why not)?

_____

_____

Which ethical principles are involved?

_____

You arrive at an interpreting assignment and find out that the client (for whom you are supposed to interpret) is your sister-in-law's niece.

What do you do?

_____

_____

Which ethical principles are involved?

_____

You arrive at an interpreting assignment wearing a tee-shirt and sandals at a nonprofit agency where many service providers wear jeans.

Is this dress acceptable for professional interpreters? Why (or why not)?

_____

_____

Which ethical principles are involved?

_____

The client is so happy for all your assistance and seems to have so many problems that you want to give her your home phone number.

Should you do so? Why (or why not)?

_____

_____

Which ethical principles are involved?

_____

You are a refugee resettlement case manager working with a family. After several incidents of domestic violence occur, you interpret for the client at a domestic violence shelter. When you get back to the agency, a co-worker asks you what happened.

Can you tell your co-worker what happened? Why or why not?

_____

_____

Which ethical principles are involved?

_____

You have an appointment at the Health Department to interpret for a nurse who is giving information about both breast feeding and bottle feeding. You tell the client that breast-feeding is much better for the baby and the mother should breastfeed.

Is this acceptable? Why (or why not)?

_____

_____

Which ethical principles are involved?

_____

You have very strong feelings about abortion (either for or against it). You are given an assignment at an abortion clinic.

Should you accept the assignment? Why (or why not)?

_____

_____

Which ethical principles are involved?

_____

A small girl has bruises. The Department of Social Services is investigating the parents for child abuse. You are aware that, in the culture of the parents, strong physical discipline is a cultural norm. In other words, many parents may strongly believe in the idea of "Spare the rod and spoil the child." A "good parent" may be expected to use physical discipline often in this culture.

Should you explain this issue to the service provider? Why (or why not)?

_____

_____

Which ethical principles are involved?

_____

A patient tells you, "Yeah, I already know I have HIV. But I can't tell my wife. She would be too upset. Hey, don't tell the doctor I said that!"

Do you break confidentiality and tell the doctor? Why (or why not?)

_____

Which ethical principles are involved?

_____

Exercise 1-i   **Ethical Dilemma Role Plays**

Note: The following scripts are in *English only*. Act them out in groups of three who speak the same language. Do not worry about positioning or other professional skills, as these will be taught in Unit 2. Think only about accuracy and what to do when you reach the ethical dilemma.

If your instructor wishes, he or she may ask you to interpret from English into English so you do not have to worry about the language differences. Otherwise, if you are the person who plays the client, you may sight translate (orally translate) the text into your target language by reading the text out loud in the other language.

SPECIAL NOTE: THE PERSON WHO PLAYS THE INTERPRETER WILL NOT LOOK AT THE SCRIPT AT ANY POINT DURING THIS EXERCISE. Only the individuals who play the *provider (Text A=Doctor, Text B=Counselor)* and *client (Text A=Patient, Text B=Domestic Violence Victim)* may see the script.

Furthermore, after the ethical dilemma there is *no script*. At that point, the interpreter will have to decide what to do and the provider and client will simply improvise for a few sentences to support whatever the interpreter decides to do. Then wrap up the role play, proceed to the second script and execute that role play with a different person playing the interpreter.

Text A   **HEALTHCARE: Car Accident**

Number of participants: 3
Roles: Doctor, patient, interpreter
Setting: HMO or private physician's office
Situation: Patient was recently in a car accident and is describing his or her injuries.

Patient: I have a lot of bruises and my neck is hurting. The police officer said I should see my doctor, and the insurance company said I might have another healthcare exam later.

Doctor: Yes, that's right. I'm glad you came in. When did the accident happen?

Patient: Early this morning, but I had to go to work. I was turning left when a car hit me. I didn't even see it coming.

Doctor: Did the airbag deploy?

Patient: Oh, yes, with a bang. And then it burst and made a funny smell and the smoke—it was terrible! Is that smoke bad for me?

Doctor: No, that's nothing to worry about. Where do you hurt?

Patient: Everywhere! But especially my neck is sore, the back here. And I have bruises on my stomach and chest. And a terrible taste in my mouth.

Doctor: That's probably just from the chemicals and dust from the airbag. That should go away. If it doesn't, let me know—but what else is wrong?

Patient: My lower back, right here. That's the worst part. I had trouble walking, today and now I'm afraid it will last a long time, my back problems. They say once you mess your back up in an accident, you can have problems for years!

Doctor: What is the pain like on a scale of 1 to 10?

Patient: Maybe—I don't know—7 or so?

Doctor: Well, we need to take pictures of the bruises for the insurance company. And I can refer you to a physical therapist, but for now you need to rest your back, put ice on your neck and I'm going to give you a prescription for pain killers and some instructions for your back.

Patient: (turns to the interpreter with a smile and whispers to the INTERPRETER, not the doctor). Really, my back's just fine. But my family is about to lose our apartment, so I'm going to screw the other guy's insurance company for all it's worth, because I really need the money. Hey, don't tell the doc I said that!

Number of Participants: 3
Roles: Counselor, domestic violence victim, interpreter
Setting: Nonprofit domestic violence center (counseling office, not the shelter)
Situation: A new client in intake has just told the story of her husband beating her up repeatedly when he drinks. She is very upset.

Client: But the thing I'm most worried about is the police came and arrested my husband last night. They're going to charge him with domestic violence—my friends tell me he could be deported.

Counselor: That's possible, but right now we don't know if—

Client: (in tears) You don't understand. I don't have papers. I can't work. If they deport him, I can't pay the rent. If he goes, they're going to throw us to the streets.

Counselor: Yes, I can see you're very worried, but—

Client: He's a good man when he doesn't drink. He works hard. It's just I make him angry when I burn things or don't pay attention to him and you have to understand we have nothing, no savings, no papers, nothing.

Counselor: I know you're in a difficult situation. But we can—

Client: And then sometimes he threatened if they arrest him he's going to have me deported so I never see the kids again. And that scares me. My children are everything to me!

Counselor: Yes, but.

Client: And I told you, he doesn't have a lawyer so I don't even know what's really going on and what's going to happen to him and to us and...

Counselor: (in frustration, turns to the INTERPRETER and says to her, speaking about the client) Does she understand a word I'm saying? Can't you just get her to *listen* to me a minute?

Exercise 1-j   Ethics Role Plays

The instructor will divide everyone into pairs. You do not need to speak the same language to act out these role plays.

   1. Read the sample role play below (Confidentiality).
   2. Then, fill in any blanks in some of the role plays below, so that the person who plays the interpreter knows what to say.
   2. Act out the role plays.
   3. After executing each role play, switch roles *before* moving onto the next role play so that both individuals have a chance to play the interpreter.

CONFIDENTIALITY

Situation: *A receptionist at a refugee resettlement agency approaches the interpreter after she interpreted the day before for a client at the Social Security office. The receptionist is aware that the client has applied for disability benefits.*

Receptionist: Mrs. Nguyen is such a sweet lady! How did it go? Do you think they will give her the SSDI? [Social Security Disability Income]

Interpreter: I'm sorry, but as a trained interpreter I'm bound by strict code of ethics, including confidentiality. So I'm afraid I can't tell you how it went.

IMPARTIALITY

Situation: *The client and the interpreter are alone while the provider leaves to fetch an application form for the client to fill out.*

Client: I'm so confused! What do you think I should do? If I accept this service, will it hurt me when I apply for citizenship?
Interpreter: That's a very good question. The provider should be here in just a moment, and you can ask her.
Client: But what do *you* think? Can't you tell me?
Interpreter:

_____
_____
_____

PROFESSIONAL BOUNDARIES

Situation: *The provider and interpreter are alone in the hallway outside the room where the client is waiting.*

Provider: Could you please explain this form to him while I check in with the next client?
Interpreter:

_____
_____
_____

Provider: But I'm really in a rush. You've done this form a million times, you could do it for the client in your sleep!
Interpreter: _____
_____
_____

CULTURAL COMPETENCE

Situation: *This conversation takes place right after the client has left an interpreted encounter.*

Provider: So what was going on in there? Do women in that culture just sit there and let men do all the talking?

Interpreter:

_____

_____

_____

Special note: Here is one example of what an interpreter might say in the situation described above. Read it for guidance; then write your own words in the lines above before you act out the role play. _Do not give cultural information about the roles of men and women in the culture, even if you think you know the culture very well._

Interpreter: I'm sorry, I'm not a cultural expert. Men and women from her culture could react in all kinds of different ways. A lot of it might depend on their beliefs and education and how they were raised. So you might want to speak to the client about this, and I'd be happy to interpret your questions.

PROFESSIONALISM

Before executing this role play, jot down some reasons that the interpreter could give the client for declining the gift and some suggestions about what the client could do instead to show her gratefulness.

Situation: *A client offers the interpreter a small but pretty gift. The interpreter thanks the client but declines, explaining that the organization has a policy against accepting gifts. The client insists. Then the interpreter gently explains the risk that she might lose her job by accepting a gift and provides other reasons not to accept.*

Other ways the client could show gratefulness:

_____

_____

Reasons not to accept the gift:

_____

_____

_____

Client: This is something very small, but I just wanted to show you my appreciation.

Interpreter [graciously declines gift]:

_____

_____

_____

Client: But how can you say no! This is so small, and no one will know. How could you hurt my feelings this way!

Interpreter [gives suggestions and reasons]:

_____
_____
_____

PROFESSIONALISM and ROLE BOUNDARIES

Situation: *The provider asks the interpreter to translate a document written in legal language. The interpreter tells the supervisor politely that s/he cannot translate the form. When the supervisor insists, the interpreter offers alternatives and then good reasons to decline. Select examples from the list below that you think would convince a provider you know in real life, and write them in the blanks below. Then act out the role play.*

Examples of alternatives to suggest (choose the ones you find most convincing)
- You might want to call the local XYZ Translation Company—they do professional legal translation.
- If you look at our state registry of court-certified interpreters, many of them do legal translation.
- The American Translators Association database at www.atanet.org has a listing in their online database of certified translators, and you can even search by zip code.
- So-and-so has done professional legal translation for us before, and I heard that management is very satisfied with her work—you could call her.

Examples of good arguments (choose the ones you find most convincing)
- I don't understand legal terminology.
- I'm not court-certified or qualified to translate.
- I have no training in translation.
- It would take hours to translate even one page properly, and there is no time.
- An inaccurate translation would put you and the agency at risk for a lawsuit.
- I would also be liable for my mistakes.
- The agency may look ridiculous if a document comes out with many errors.
- Interpreting involves a very different set of skills than those for translation.
- Federal regulations might require a qualified translator.
- The client might not understand my inaccurate translation.
- The client may make poor decisions due to my inaccurate translation.

Provider: Please translate this for us and have it done by next week. It's pretty urgent.

Interpreter: I'm very sorry. I know this is an important document and I'd love to help you with it, but you might want to call [give a suggestion] because I'm not a qualified translator and I don't know legal terminology. I could make serious mistakes.

Provider: Oh, come on. You're a great translator!

Interpreter: Actually I'm an interpreter, not a translator. And _____

_____

_____

_____

ACCURACY AND COMPLETENESS

Situation. *An invisible provider has just said something the client does not like. Note: This role play requires only two participants. Just pretend that a provider is present. Also, the person playing the client will sight translate the text into his/her other language.*

Client (sight translate the following text, then say it out loud to an invisible provider): I don't care what you say. I'm not going to do it. Fuck you.

Interpreter (interprets accurately into English): I don't care what you say. I'm not going to do it. Fuck you.

Note: "Fuck you" has many possible ways of being expressed in another language. Use any offensive, colloquial expression that respects the language register and meaning. The interpreter should not soften the language.

Exercise I-k (optional)   Ethical Violations

In small groups, let everyone write down two examples of ethical violations they have committed in the past (if they have any past interpreting experience). Then each person should write down what he or she would do differently now. After this is done, discuss these situations with the other participants in the group to see if they agree.

Ethical violation:

_____

_____

What I would do differently now:

_____

_____

_____

Ethical violation:

_____

_____

What I would do differently now:

_____

_____

_____

Exercise I-I (optional)   Sector-Specific Ethics Role Plays

Note: All these role plays are for two individuals only. They are conducted in *English*.

TEXT A   HEALTHCARE: Prenatal

Number of Participants: 2
Roles: Supervisor and a bilingual employee in Healthcare Records
Setting: A hospital prenatal clinic

Supervisor: Look, I have to send you down to Radiology right now. There's some kind of situation down there and they need an interpreter this minute.

Bilingual employee: I'm sorry, I feel very comfortable doing prenatal but I don't know the terminology for Radiology.

Supervisor: But this is important.

Bilingual employee: Then it will be much safer for them to pick up the phone and call a staff interpreter or a telephone interpreter. I'm sure you wouldn't want the hospital liable for my mistakes.

TEXT B   HUMAN SERVICES: Office of Human Rights

Number of Participants: 2
Roles: Investigator; interpreter
Setting: Local Office of Human Rights
Situation: The investigator has just finished taking a detailed statement from a client who is accusing his former boss of discrimination on the basis of his country of origin. The client is in the lobby.

Investigator: (to the interpreter, who is also a bilingual secretary) I'm going to do the write-up now. Here are the forms he needs to sign. You explain them to him.

Interpreter: But if I'm going to sight translate the forms the client may have questions for you.

Investigator: You know all this stuff. I don't have time.

Interpreter: But now that I've been trained as an interpreter, I know that I shouldn't be sight translating documents that I don't fully understand. I am not a trained investigator, and I need you to be there when we—

Investigator: The client can just come to me when you're finished with his questions. I don't have time for this right now. You take care of it. (Investigator tries to leave the room.)

(As the interpreter, you should come up with the strongest possible arguments *to convince the investigator to remain present*.)

29

TEXT C   EDUCATION: ARD Meeting

Number of Participants: 2
Roles: Volunteer language bank interpreter; parent
Setting: An elementary school
Situation: A parent who is waiting alone with the interpreter, who will be interpreting for an Admission, Review and Dismissal (ARD) meeting about a child's special education services.

Parent: I don't agree that my child needs special education services. What should I do?

Interpreter: I'm very sorry. This is an important question, but as the interpreter I'm really not allowed to give advice. I'll be happy to interpret your question to the teacher or principal when the ARD meeting begins. It's their job to give you all the information to make the best decision for your child. I'm only here as the interpreter. That's the best help I can give you—to be your voice so you can help your child.

TEXT D   HUMAN SERVICES: Housing

Number of Participants: 2
Roles: Applicant for subsidized housing; interpreter
Setting: Housing office

Applicant: When we go in there, please explain everything to the lady. You know everything about my case, you know how to make it sound good. And I really need that housing.

Interpreter: I'll be happy to interpret, but unfortunately I can't explain anything. The staff member will ask you questions to be sure she understands your case properly, and I'll interpret everything you say. That way you can get the best service.

TEXT E   EDUCATION: Head Start

Number of Participants: 2
Roles: Parent, interpreter
Setting: A Head Start program

Parent: [speak in the other language if desired] Can you help me fill out this form, it's driving me crazy!

Interpreter: I'm sorry. I'm only allowed to help with forms when someone from the office is here to answer your questions. Let me get Ms Brown to help you, and I'll be happy to interpret for you.

Exercise 1-m (optional)   Case Study

In pairs, read the following true story told to one of the authors by the interpreter. Then answer the questions below.

One day an interpreter was sent by the police to interpret for a woman who had just been stabbed in the chest. She arrived with the paramedics.

Through the interpreter, the woman told the police she had been stabbed by a thief who came to rob the house, and the interpreter faithfully interpreted everything she said. As they waited for the police officers to interview her, the woman whispered to the interpreter, "You are my sister (she meant, "my friend"). I'll tell you the truth. It was my husband who stabbed me. But don't tell the police."

Trained as an interpreter by the Red Cross, the interpreter knew she must respect confidentiality. She also knew that if she violated confidentiality, the story would spread all over her local ethnic community and the interpreter would probably be shunned by the entire community. She was the only interpreter for that language community and feared they would lose her, and she would lose their trust forever.

However, the woman had a two-year-old daughter. As she looked into the eyes of that little girl, the interpreter knew in her heart that she could not respect the woman's wishes. For the woman's sake, and above all for the tiny daughter, the interpreter decided to break confidentiality and tell the truth to the police.

When she gently informed the woman before she did so, the woman wept and pleaded with her not to reveal the truth. So the interpreter felt terrible but told the police everything she had heard.

The police immediately left the house to look for the husband. They found him hiding around the corner, holding the bloody knife—waiting for an opportunity to come back and kill his wife. The police arrested him. He went to prison, and the woman was safe. This event became public knowledge in that community.

The wife was so grateful to the interpreter that instead of saying how bad the interpreter was for betraying her trust, she spread the word throughout the community that the interpreter had saved her life.

1. Did the interpreter violate confidentiality? Why or why not?

_____

_____

2. Did she act ethically? Why or why not?

_____

_____

Exercise 1-n (optional)   Following a Code of Ethics

This exercise may be used in class or executed as a home assignment.

FOLLOWING A CODE OF ETHICS	
Confidentiality	1. Can you tell your husband about the dramatic interpreting experience you had today? What exactly *can* you say?
	2. The patient or client says, "I'm pregnant. But don't tell the caseworker I told you that!" Should you tell?
	3. Under what situations might an interpreter have to violate confidentiality?
	4. If a client or patient discloses *outside* the session (where no one else can hear) that she is a victim of domestic violence, and forbids you to tell anyone about it, may you disclose this information?
	5. What information about your interpreting experiences can you share at a training or professional in-service?
	6. How can you avoid being left alone with a client or patient?
Accuracy	1. The doctor spoke so fast you didn't catch everything. What do you do?
	2. The client rambles on and on and on. Do you interpret everything?
	3. The provider is speaking in a very high register that the client doesn't understand. Do you simplify the language? Why or why not?
	4. During the session, the provider says comments about the client that are rude, bigoted and/or racist (thinking that you will not interpret them). Do you interpret the comments? Soften them? Ask the provider to change what is being said?
	5. The client gets angry and swears. Do you interpret every word? What do you do if you don't know how to say those words in English?
	6. Do you interpret body language? Why or why not?
	7. If more than one person is speaking, how do you handle the situation?
Impartiality	1. What do you do during the session if a client turns to you and asks, "I'm confused—what do *you* think I should do?"
	2. Should the interpreter's voice be neutral?
	3. You arrive and find you know the client (slightly). What do you do?
	4. If the client is about to make a poor decision with serious consequences, can you intervene to guide the client to a better choice?
	5. You are asked to interpret something that you know to be a lie. What do you do?
Role Boundaries	1. You are a bilingual employee. During the session, your colleague turns to you and asks you a question about the client. What do you do?
	2. After the session, a client asks you to make a phone call to social services or to help reduce a hospital bill. What do you do?

	4. Your colleague asks you to drive the client to the next appointment. What do you say?
Cultural Competence	1. Which cultures should the interpreter try to learn about?
	2. Should the interpreter explain cultural issues during a session? Why or why not?
	3. The client is taking a cultural home remedy that the nurse doesn't understand. Do you explain what that remedy is and why the patient is taking it?
	4. The service system (healthcare, schools, or social services) is completely different in the client's country, which is causing great confusion in the session. Do you explain that service system to the provider?
	5. The client cannot understand next steps because the service system is too complicated. The provider does not seem to be aware. How do you handle it?
Respect	1. How do you show respect to all parties?
	2. If your language has a formal and informal level of address (e.g. tu/Ud), which one do you use when you interpret?
	3. A provider speaks rudely and dismissively about a parent in your presence, making you angry at her cultural insensitivity and attitude. You don't want to interpret for her anymore because you don't respect her now. What will you do?
Advocacy	1. What does advocacy mean?
	2. Under what circumstances may the interpreter engage in advocacy?
	3. Before advocating, what should the interpreter try first?
	4. What are the risks of advocating?
	5. If the situation is very serious but the client says, "Don't do it," can you still advocate?
Professional Development	1. What kinds of professional development are available for community interpreters?
	2. What basic resources should the interpreter procure?
	3. What are the best ways to practice interpreting skills after training?
Professionalism	1. You have been interpreting about five minutes, and already three or four words have come up that you do not know. What do you do?
	2. You work for a nonprofit agency that assists immigrants but are asked to accompany a patient to the hospital Emergency Room. You don't know healthcare terminology. What should you do?
	3. A client offers a dish of home-made pastries to show her gratefulness to you. How do you handle the offer?
	4. You do such a wonderful job that your client *insists* that you accept a silver bracelet from her country. Refusing a gift is culturally problematic: she will be so offended that she may never return to the service. What do you say?
	5. At the last minute, you cannot go to interpret as scheduled. You have a friend who interprets. Can you send her instead? Why or why not?

Exercise 1-o (optional)   Mini Case Studies

EDUCATION: Confidentiality

You interpret at various schools in your jurisdiction. You interpret at a Board hearing regarding a student's suspension from school. The next day, a teacher who was not present at the hearing asks, "How did it go yesterday about Roberto?" Can you tell her about Roberto's case?

Factors to consider:
- How much of the information is public knowledge?
- Is this teacher one of Roberto's teachers?
- Is she part of an instructional team that works closely with Roberto?
- What is the official policy about confidentiality at that school?
- Was the interpreter given specific guidance on the issue?

SOCIAL SERVICES: Accuracy and Cultural Competence

The client has only a second-grade education. He curses. You know this will offend the Department of Social Services caseworker. After interpreting the offensive words, do you educate the client on appropriate language to use in American social service settings?

Factors to consider:
- Is it appropriate to give the client a chance to restate what was said in less offensive language?
- Can the interpreter alert the caseworker that it might be helpful for the caseworker to educate the client about American social service settings?
- Are caseworkers at this agency generally helpful and client-friendly or are they unlikely to provide the client with helpful guidance?
- Is the client abusive to you too? If so, may you withdraw?

HEALTHCARE: Professionalism

You start to introduce yourself to the patient when the doctor brushes you off and says, "I'm very rushed. Let me get started here." What do you do?

Factors to consider:
- Do you work with this doctor regularly?
- Has the patient worked with a professional interpreter before?
- Will you be able to take the doctor aside at another time and respectfully explain the importance of introductions for new patients?
- Is this patient worried and tense? Is she confused about what is going on? Does she need to know who you are and how an interpreted session will proceed?
- Is the patient going to start talking to you instead of the doctor?
- Is the doctor's brusque manner upsetting the patient? Might it erode trust, making the patient grow dependent on the interpreter?

HUMAN AND SOCIAL SERVICES: Role Boundaries

You are a bilingual caseworker at a refugee resettlement agency. Your supervisor asks you to drive the client to the Department of Social Services. Professional interpreters are not typically supposed to drive clients around because it may erode professional boundaries and lead the client to disclose personal information that is problematic to keep confidential. Do you refuse to drive the client or agree to do so?

Factors to consider:
- Is driving clients to appointments a part of your job description?
- Do other caseworkers there also have to do it?
- Will you get in trouble or lose your job if you refuse to drive the client?
- Does the client have access to other types of transportation?
- Are you able to maintain professional boundaries while driving alone with the client?

HUMAN AND SOCIAL SERVICES: Impartiality

You are asked to interpret for a woman who was followed at a supermarket by an employee and accused of stealing sunglasses. (She had not). She is filing a human rights complaint. When you arrive at the human rights office to interpret, the woman turns out to be your neighbor down the street.

Factors to consider:
- When you declare the conflict, how do the investigator and client feel?
- Do they both wish you to interpret anyway?
- Do you feel comfortable interpreting for her?
- Would knowing this woman in such a casual way affect your ability to interpret for her accurately and well?
- Are you likely to interpret for her again?
- Would the fact that she knows where to find you lead her to start asking you to interpret for free?

EDUCATION: Professionalism

A teacher asks you to call a parent to set up an Admission, Review and Dismissal (ARD) meeting. The teacher expects you to explain on the phone what an ARD meeting is to the parent. Do you accept? Do you ask the teacher to be present when you make that call? Do you explain the ARD process yourself or ask the teacher to do so?

Factors to consider:
- Were you given training in special education and IEP/ARD meetings and services?
- Is it a part of your work to make such explanations in English to native-born parents?
- Do you make such phone calls frequently?
- Do you have the professional competence and qualifications needed to answer any questions that the parent might ask you?
- Is it part of your job description to provide parent education or explanations?

HEALTHCARE: Accuracy

A nurse hands you a video on diabetes and says, "Here. I know the language is way too technical for this patient. Just tell him basically what the video says." Then she walks away. Should you summarize the video or politely tell the nurse why you refuse to do so?

Factors to consider:
- Is health education a part of your job description?
- Do you have a clinical background? Were you trained to provide education about diabetes?
- Are you primarily an interpreter or a community health worker?
- What is your skill level with this healthcare vocabulary?
- Does your "gut" tell you that your explanations of the video may cause problems for the patient to understand correctly?

ANY SERVICE: Professionalism

On your way to an interpreting assignment, you get caught in bad traffic caused by an accident. You will be very late. Should you call the provider and offer to send someone else you know to interpret?

Factors to consider:
- Is the "someone else" a trained, qualified interpreter?
- Is the "someone else" authorized and able to interpret for domestic violence cases?
- Were you sent by a language company or interpreter service who should handle this?
- Is there a bilingual employee on site who speaks your language who could step in for you at the last minute?

ANY SERVICE: Professionalism

A client for whom you recently interpreted is so grateful for your help that she brings you a pretty porcelain plate from her home country. In her culture, to refuse such a gift would be a very deep insult. Can you accept the plate?

Factors to consider:
- Does your agency have a policy on accepting small gifts?
- Have you discussed the cultural issues concerning gifts with your supervisors?
- Will refusing this gift cause trouble for you in your cultural community?
- Will your agency accept gifts if they stay on display in the office, for everyone to share?
- If you tell the client, "In the U.S. we're not supposed to accept gifts like this. My agency is very strict about the gifts policy, and I might lose my job for accepting one," would the client understand and be more accepting of your refusal?
- Can you redirect the client's gratefulness, e.g., by suggesting some other way of showing appreciation? (Examples: give the gift to a charity, write a thank you letter, make a donation to a nonprofit, etc.)

UNIT 2 INTERPRETER SKILLS

OBJECTIVE 2.1
Execute an interpreted session.

2.1 (a) List the steps to execute an interpreted session.
2.1 (b) Discuss and select appropriate modes of interpreting.
2.1 (c) Practice interpreting in consecutive and simultaneous modes.
2.1 (d) Demonstrate basic sight translation skills.

Exercise 2-a   **Steps of an Interpreted Session**

The instructor will play a film vignette or demonstrate a brief interpreted session from beginning to end. As you watch, see if you can identify the steps of an interpreted session and list them in the lines below.

_____

_____

_____

_____

_____

_____

Exercise 2-b (optional)   Preparation

You are a contract interpreter who has just been asked to perform an interpreting assignment in three days. Choose ONE assignment from the list below. Then, in pairs, answer questions 1 and 2.

  a) **Healthcare:** The appointment of a cancer patient with his oncologist.
  b) **Education:** A school Board hearing about a student who hit another student in class.
  c) **Human services:** A domestic violence center group session for men who batter women.

1. What information do you need to collect ahead of time about the appointment?

_____

_____

_____

_____

2. How should you prepare for this assignment? (Offer details such as resources, specific dictionaries, websites and strategies.)

_____

_____

_____

_____

Exercise 2-c   Selecting Modes

Select the appropriate mode for the situations below from this list: consecutive, simultaneous, whisper interpreting, sight translation or summary.

1. A doctor sees a patient for a routine physical. _____

2. A Back to School Night or immigration clinic is held where most participants speak English. Two smaller groups speak Spanish and Korean. _____

3. The customer must fill out a financial qualification form. _____

4. In the Emergency Room, a gunshot victim is bleeding so badly that the doctor refuses to be interrupted while asking the patient questions. _____

5. During a parent-teacher interview, the mother, father and aunt get into an argument with the child. All four are speaking at once and will not calm down. _____

Exercise 2-d   Consecutive Mode Skills Building

In this exercise, like other skills-based exercises, the interpreter must never read the text that is being interpreted. The person who plays the interpreter must always close his or her workbook.

Take turns executing the texts below. For Text A, Partner 1 will play the interpreter and must close this workbook. Partner 2 will read Text A out loud, *pausing after every sentence* to allow time to interpret. Partner 3 will observe the session and write down answers to the questions following Text A in the workbook of *Partner 1 (the interpreter)*.

Now proceed to Text B and do the same. (If this class is for healthcare interpreting, repeat Text A.) Now Partner 2 will play the interpreter; Partner 3 will read Text B out loud; and Partner 1 will observe and note down any comments to give to Partner 2.

TEXT A   HEALTHCARE

1. Are you aware that a rectal temperature over 100.4°F accompanied by vomiting or poor feeding may mean that your baby is very sick?
2. When was your last eye exam?
3. This prescription is a combination of female hormones that prevent ovulation.
4. How long have you been having pain in your lower back?
5. If you have any questions about your medication, the pharmacist will be happy to assist you.
6. What was the date of your last period?
7. Have there been any major changes or stresses in your life since your last visit? Could you please describe them?
8. Has anyone who ever lived in your house or cared for your children had a positive skin test for tuberculosis (TB) or a case of active TB?
9. Yes, you're right, there's more radiation from a CT-scan than a typical X-ray, but it's still minor and nothing to be concerned about.
10. I'm sorry to tell you your wife has miscarried.
11. We might have to refer you a dental specialist, because your chronic jaw pain might be a sign of TMJ [temperomandibular joint disorder].

TEXT B   EDUCATION

1. Yes, I'm afraid the HSA [high school assessment] requirement does apply to students like your daughter with Limited English Proficiency.
2. We'd like to refer your son to the Child Find program for testing because we suspect he has ADHD [Attention Deficit Hyperactivity Disorder].
3. The Board hearing about your child's suspension will be held on April 30 at 8:00 p.m., and we can arrange for an interpreter to be there.
4. The school nurse says your daughter has a fever. Will you be able to pick her up from school right away?
5. Of course, I'd be happy to explain what an ARD [Admission, Review and Dismissal] meeting is about.
6. Yes, you're right, the SAT prep program offered by our school carries a fee. But we have some funds you could apply for to cover that fee—would you like a copy of the application form?
7. The school counselor won't be in today and would like to reschedule your daughter's appointment to discuss college scholarships.
8. I'm sorry, but the police are here right now to question your son about that incident in the locker room.
9. If you haven't reviewed our inclement weather policy you'll need to understand it so you know when our sports events are canceled.

10. I also suggest you register at www.schoolsout.com if you have access to a computer at home because then you won't have to listen to a radio or TV to learn about school closings.
11. One purpose of a parent-teacher conference is to discuss your child's progress and make sure that you're aware of everything you can do to support your child.
12. We can appreciate how hard it must be to keep up with your child's homework. Did you know we have an after-school homework club with volunteer tutors and a tutoring hotline?

Exercise 2-e   **Consecutive Mode Role Plays**

Execute the following role plays as the instructor advises you. Ideally, you will act them out in groups of four with three people playing the roles and one person observing and noting down everything that the interpreter performs well while also noting any errors, omissions, additions or changes to the message. (This fourth person is called a language coach. The instructor may have professional language coaches available instead.)

Remember: THE PERSON WHO PLAYS THE INTERPRETER MUST NOT LOOK AT THE SCRIPT and must keep this workbook closed during the role play.

The language coach can use the model in the box below as a guide for noting down feedback.

Comments on everything the interpreter performed well or smoothly:
_____
_____

Number of times the interpreter *omitted* something in the text (did not interpret it): _____
Number of times the interpreter *added* something to the text: _____
Number of times the interpreter *changed* the text: _____
Number of grammatical errors: _____

Other errors: (specify)
_____
_____
_____

Which parts appeared more difficult to interpret? Why?
_____
_____

Note any other comments or suggestions:
_____
_____

TEXT A **HEALTHCARE: Miscarriage (Aborto espontáneo)**

Spanish-English

Parent: Estoy buscando a mi hija. Recibí una llamada telefónica avisándome que la habían traído aquí a la clínica.

Nurse: She's in the emergency room.

Parent: ¿Cómo está? ¿Sabe que está embarazada?

Nurse: Yes, we know, but apparently she miscarried.

Parent: ¿Está seguro? ¿Está seguro de que está hablando de mi hija?

Nurse: Yes, her name is Alana, right?

Parent: Si, así es. ¿Dónde está?

Nurse: As I said, she's in the ER, and she's still heavily medicated.

Parent: ¿Qué pasó? ¿Por qué la trajeron?

Nurse: Apparently she was found at her home, very sick. When she arrived here, she was under the influence of medications. She overdosed with over-the-counter medications.

English only

Parent: I'm trying to find my daughter. I got a phone call telling me that she was brought to this clinic.

Nurse: She's in the emergency room.

Parent: How is she doing. She's pregnant, did you know?

Nurse: Yes, we know, but apparently she miscarried.

Parent: Are you sure? Are you talking about my daughter?

Nurse: Yes, her name is Alana, right?

Parent: That's right, where is she?

Nurse: As I said, she's in the ER, and she's still heavily medicated.

Parent: What happened? Why was she brought here?

Nurse: Apparently she was found at her home, very sick. When she arrived here, she was under the influence of medications. She overdosed with over-the-counter medications.

Client: Señorita, me da mucha pena pero necesito ayuda.

Client: Miss, I'm very embarrassed but I need some help.

Information and Referral specialist (IRS): Yes, how may I help you?

Information and Referral specialist (IRS): Yes, how may I help you?

Client: Bueno, es que mi esposo nos dejó y estoy criando cuatro hijos yo sola. Tengo que limpiar casas para tener una casa, pero no me alcanza para la comida. Los chicos mayores entienden que no pueden comer mucho pero los menores no entienden. ¿Dónde puedo recibir ayuda?

Client: Well, my husband left us and I'm raising four children by myself. I have to clean houses to keep a roof over our heads but I'm coming up short of food. The older kids understand not to eat that much but the younger ones don't get it. Where can I get help?

IRS: You need to go to a food bank and maybe get food stamps, too. Were your children born in the U.S.?

IRS: You need to go to a food bank and maybe get food stamps, too. Were your children born in the U.S.?

Client: Sí, ¿acaso el banco de comida y las estampillas de comida son la misma cosa?

Client: Sí. Is food bank the same thing as food stamps?

IRS: Oh no, no. A food bank is a charitable organization that distributes mostly donated food to a wide variety of agencies who give it to the people who need it. Each food bank has different rules, and they distribute the food on different dates. They'll give you a bag of food. The food might not be exactly what you are used to eating so you might have to make some changes.

IRS: Oh no, no. A food bank is a charitable organization that distributes mostly donated food to a wide variety of agencies who give it to the people who need it. Each food bank has different rules, and they distribute the food on different dates. They'll give you a bag of food. The food might not be exactly what you are used to eating so you might have to make some changes.

Client: ¿Y qué son las estampillas de comida?

Client: And what are food stamps?

IRS: The food stamp program helps low-income people buy food. It's a federal government program run by state or local agencies. You need to go to Social Services to apply. Children born in the U.S. qualify for food stamps.

IRS: The food stamp program helps low-income people buy food. It's a federal government program run by state or local agencies. You need to go to Social Services to apply. Children born in the U.S. qualify for food stamps.

Client: ¿Puede darme la dirección por favor?

Client: Can you please give me the address?

TEXT C   **EDUCATION: Sex Offense**

Assistant Principal (AP): Sir/ma'am, your son has been taken out of the classroom. A female classmate said he had touched her inappropriately.

Parent: ¿Cómo es posible? ¿Qué hizo? ¡Yo siempre le he enseñado buenos modales y buena educación!

AP: I'm sure you've raised him well, but unfortunately, a female student reported him and we need to refer this to the administration. They have to follow up with the disciplinary committee and even possibly with the police.

Parent: ¿Qué fue lo que hizo exactamente?

AP: He touched a girl's behind while she was going up the stairs. This is considered sexual harassment or assault. The police are meeting with her to determine the offense.

Parent: ¿Está seguro que la niña no hizo algo que causara esto? No puedo creer que mi hijo hizo esto.

AP: We find it hard to believe ourselves because he's never caused any kind of problem. This is a surprise to us as well.

Parent: ¿Puedo hablar con él? Necesito oírlo directamente de él.

AP: Well, I'm not sure. He's in a separate room waiting to hear from the police.

Parent: ¡Pero esto quiere decir que usted piensa que el es culpable! ¡Necesito hablar con él!

AP: I don't think I can allow this right now.

Parent: ¿¡Como?! Yo soy el padre y estamos en la escuela. Yo tengo el derecho de hablar con mi hijo; usted no lo puede detener así. Yo exijo hablar con mi hijo ahora mismo!

Assistant Principal (AP): Sir/ma'am, your son has been taken out of the classroom. A female classmate said he had touched her inappropriately.

Parent: How could this be? What did he do? I've always taught him good manners!

AP: I'm sure you've raised him well, but unfortunately, a female student reported him and we need to refer this to the administration. They have to follow up with the disciplinary committee and even possibly with the police.

Parent: What exactly did he do?

AP: He touched a girl's behind while she was going up the stairs. This is considered sexual harassment or assault. The police are meeting with her to determine the offense.

Parent: Are you sure the girl didn't do something to cause this? I can't believe that my son did this.

AP: We find it hard to believe ourselves because he's never caused any kind of problem. This is a surprise to us as well.

Parent: Can I talk to him? I need to hear it directly from him.

AP: Well, I'm not sure. He's in a separate room waiting to hear from the police.

Parent: But this means that you believe he's guilty! I need to talk with him!

AP: I don't think I can allow this right now.

Parent: What!? I'm the parent and we're in the school. I have the right to talk to my son; you can't hold him like this. I demand to speak with him right now!

Exercise 2-f   **Simultaneous Mode Practice**

The instructor will divide you into pairs. One of you will select one or more of the following texts and read it out loud to the person who plays the interpreter, who will interpret the text in simultaneous mode. If you speak the same language, you can then offer the interpreter feedback and switch roles. Again, use the model below as a guide for noting down feedback to give the interpreter.

Comments on everything the interpreter performed well or smoothly:

_____

_____

Number of times the interpreter *omitted* something in the text (did not interpret it): _____

Number of times the interpreter *added* something to the text: _____

Number of times the interpreter *changed* the text: _____

Number of grammatical errors: _____

Other errors: (specify)

_____

_____

_____

Which parts appeared more difficult to interpret? Why?

_____

_____

Note any other comments or suggestions:

_____

_____

TEXT A   **EDUCATION: Special Education**

Mr. Amilcar, we understand that your child is in Special Education and that you have concerns regarding the new testing procedures. You want to know why your child has to take the Standards of Learning tests to graduate—the SOLs. Well, let me explain this to you. No child with a disability may be exempted from all the SOL tests at any given grade level. That said, the IEP [Individualized Education Plan] team may determine that the child will not participate in one or more of the individual tests. In cases like this, the IEP team is required to state why the particular test is not appropriate and how the child will be assessed in that academic area. When the IEP team determines that the student doesn't meet the criteria for participation in the alternate assessment, the team has to determine the extent to which the student will participate in the SOL assessment.

You shouldn't worry about your child. The IEP team will look into his case and will make a determination about what's best for your child.

TEXT B   HEALTHCARE: HIV

Mrs. [make up a last name] let me explain what HIV is. We know the news is upsetting for you, so let's be clear. First, HIV stands for Human Immunodeficiency virus, and it's the virus that causes Acquired Immunodeficiency Syndrome (AIDS). You can become infected with HIV by exchanging blood, semen or vaginal secretions with a person who's infected with the virus, for example, by having sex or sharing needles with that person. A pregnant woman infected with HIV can also pass the virus to the baby at birth or it can happen after birth through her breast milk. HIV attacks your body's immune system so that you are less able to fight off germs and diseases.

You should know that the symptoms of HIV vary but for the first 7 to 10 years of HIV infection or much longer, there may be no symptoms at all. If you take the medicine we're going to prescribe for you, you might be perfectly fine. When symptoms do appear, they'll be different from person to person. Some of the symptoms that many people experience are things like night sweats, fever, extreme weight loss, diarrhea, fatigue, nausea, vomiting, swollen lymph glands, headaches, and persistent dry cough. The last stage of HIV disease is AIDS, when many life-threatening infections can cause serious disability or even death. I'm afraid there's no cure for HIV infection, but there are some effective drugs to manage it and because you're in such good health to start with it's possible you may stay healthy for years or even decades. But it's very, very important to follow the regimen we're about to prescribe.

TEXT C   HUMAN SERVICES: Child Support

Mr. Snechty, the amount of child support in this state is determined using guidelines established by state law. These guidelines are based on each parent's monthly income and the amount of time the child is cared for by each parent. If it goes to court, the court makes a decision about how much child support you should pay, and the court will consider income from all your sources of income, whether or not you reported it or it was taxed under federal law. What we consider your income can come in the form of money, property, or services. Let me give you some examples of what income means:

- Wages from a job
- Tips
- Commissions
- Bonuses
- Self-employment earnings
- Unemployment benefits
- Disability and workers' compensation
- Interest

- Dividends
- Rental income
- Social Security or pensions

Now, we don't want it to go to court. But if you don't pay child support, it will go to court, and the court has the authority to order deducting payments from each parent's gross monthly income to ensure child support.

DISCUSSION

How does simultaneous mode feel different from consecutive mode?

_____

_____

Were you able to incorporate some of the suggested techniques discussed in class?

_____

_____

What improvements have you noted since trying out the first simultaneous exercise?

_____

_____

Was your interpretation accurate and complete? Why or why not?

_____

_____

What technique so far has helped you the most to be accurate and complete?

_____

_____

How could you practice at home to improve your simultaneous interpreting skills, in case you need them in your work?

_____

_____

Exercise 2-g   Role Plays for Simultaneous Mode Practice

Act out the following role plays according to the directions given by your instructor.

TEXT A   HEALTHCARE: Drug Rehab Center
(Centro de Rehabilitación de Drogadicción)

Spanish-English

Client: Vengo a recoger jeringas para la semana.

Provider: Sorry, the needle exchange program ended.

Client: ¿Cómo pueden hacer eso? Se supone que esto debe parar el SIDA.

Provider: The government decided to end the program, and frankly our finances are in trouble and we have fewer donations as well. There's really nothing we can do. I'm sorry.

Client: ¡Pero he estado viniendo desde no se hace cuanto!

Provider: Our needle exchange program was a success for years, and we think it really helped to prevent AIDS. Unfortunately, we ran into trouble.

Client: ¡Chinga tu ma! Te las estás guardando. ¡Sácalas, hombre!

English only

Client: I'm here to pick up needles for the week.

Provider: Sorry, the needle exchange program ended.

Client: How can they do this? I thought this was supposed to stop AIDS.

Provider: The government decided to end the program, and frankly our finances are in trouble and we have fewer donations as well. There's really nothing we can do. I'm sorry.

Client: But I've been coming here since I don't know when.

Provider: Our needle exchange program was a success for years, and we think it really helped to prevent AIDS. Unfortunately, we ran into trouble.

Client: Screw you, motherfucker! You've got them here. Get 'em out, man!

Client: Señor [Señora/ Señorita], necesito hablar con alguien.

Caseworker: How may I help you?

Client: Necesito un lugar donde pueda quedarme con mis hijos. Mi esposo entregó el apartamento y no tengo dónde estar con mis hijos.

Caseworker: And where is your husband?

Client: El nos dejó y se fue a vivir con su otro hijo a Indiana.

Caseworker: But he has responsibilities as a father. He has to pay child support, and you need to file papers so he continues to support his family.

Client: ¡Ese es un bueno para nada! Si no me dió antes, ¿como me va a dar ahora? Por favor, señor, mire, mis hijos están en la escuela pero cuando lleguen del bus, no va a haber dónde ir.

Caseworker: Ok, let's see. How many children? Let me see if we have space. You have to fill out quite a bit of paper work. Do you have an I.D.?

Client: Tengo tres niños, uno de 14, otro de 13 y otro de 9. Le tengo que decir que mi hijo menor tiene un problema de no poder sentarse quieto. El tiene que moverse cada rato. La escuela me dice que tiene algo como DH.

Caseworker: Well ma'am, in that case this shelter isn't the right one for your family. I'll have to refer you to

Client: Excuse me, sir/miss/madam. I need to speak with someone.

Caseworker: How may I help you?

Client: I need a place where I can stay with my children. My husband turned in the keys to the apartment, and now I don't have a place for my children.

Caseworker: And where is your husband?

Client: He left us and moved with his other son to Indiana.

Caseworker: But he has responsibilities as a father. He has to pay child support, and you need to file papers so he continues to support his family

Client: That guy, he's a good-for-nothing! Why would he give us anything now if he never gave us anything before? Please, sir, listen, my kids are in school now and when they get off the bus, there won't be a place for them to go.

Caseworker: Ok, let's see. How many children? Let me see if we have space. You have to fill out quite a bit of paper work. Do you have an I.D.?

Client: I have three children 14, 13 and 9 years old. I have to warn you the youngest has a problem, he can't sit still, he has to move all the time. The school says he has something like DH.

Caseworker: Well ma'am, in that case this shelter isn't the right one for your family. I'll have to refer you to another one. Over there, they'll be able to place you in a room that's appropriate for your children. Can I see your I.D.?

Client: ¿Y para qué quiere mi I.D. si ya me va a mandar al otro shelter?

Caseworker: I need to open a case and refer you there. I can also call for help with transportation.

Client: ¿Y en este otro lugar, hay bolos y drogados?

Caseworker: No ma'am, we try very hard to keep our shelters "clean." We have strict rules and sanctions and if someone breaks them, then the person will have to leave. Now, may I see your I.D.?

Client: Bueno, es que tengo miedo, mire mi licencia no es de este estado, es de otro pero usted sabe que ya es más difícil sacar el I.D. en este estado.

Caseworker: Mmmm, so your I.D. says you're a resident of another state. Here at the Y, we can't process the case for request for shelter; we have to refer you back to your state.

Client: No señor, yo siempre he vivido acá, es solo que usted sabe que es difícil sacar el I.D. aquí.

Caseworker: Sorry ma'am, I can't open a case here; I will have to refer you to another Y.

Client: Señor[a/ita], usted no entiende y no sabe nada. ¡Pensé que acá eran buenas personas!

---

another one. Over there, they'll be able to place you in a room that's appropriate for your children. Can I see your I.D.?

Client: And why do you want my I.D. if you're going to send me to the other shelter?

Caseworker: I need to open a case and refer you there. I can also call for help with transportation.

Client: And in this place are there boozers and druggies?

Caseworker: No ma'am, we try very hard to keep our shelters "clean." We have strict rules and sanctions and if someone breaks them, then the person will have to leave. Now, may I see your I.D.?

Client: Well, see I am a little scared. You see, my license is not from this state, it's from another state but you know how hard it is to get one in this state.

Caseworker: Mmmm, so your I.D. says you're a resident of another state. Here at the Y, we can't process the case for request for shelter; we have to refer you back to your state.

Client: No, no, I've always lived here; it's just hard to get the I.D. here.

Caseworker: Sorry ma'am, I can't open a case here; I will have to refer you to another Y.

Client: Sir [ma'am], you don't understand, you know nothing. I thought you were good people in here!

Exercise 2-h **Sight Translation Practice**

In pairs, take turns sight translating any of the following texts that you are instructed to select and give each other constructive feedback on your performance. Remember: sight translation is more difficult than consecutive mode (and even simultaneous mode in certain respects). Be kind to each other and supportive.

Again, use the same model as before to give your partner helpful feedback.

Comments on everything the interpreter performed well or smoothly:

_____
_____

Number of times the interpreter *omitted* something (did not orally translate it): _____
Number of times the interpreter *added* something to the text: _____
Number of times the interpreter *changed* the text: _____
Number of grammatical errors: _____

Other errors: (specify)

_____
_____
_____

Which parts appeared more difficult to interpret? Why?

_____
_____

Note any other comments or suggestions:

_____
_____

TEXT A **HEALTHCARE: Discharge Instructions**

Discharge Instructions for Chronic Obstructive Pulmonary Disease (COPD)

You have been diagnosed with chronic obstructive pulmonary disease (COPD). COPD is a name given to a group of diseases. These diseases limit the flow of air in and out of your lungs, and they make it difficult for you to breathe. With COPD, you may be more likely to get lung infections. COPD included diseases like chronic bronchitis and emphysema and it's most often caused by smoking cigarettes heavily for a long period of time. If you are still smoking, the first thing you should do if at all possible is to quit smoking.

1. Break the smoking habit.
    o   Enroll in a program to stop smoking. These programs increase your chances of success.
    o   Ask your doctor for prescription medications and other methods to help you quit smoking.
    o   Ask any family members at home to quit smoking.
    o   Don't allow anyone to smoke inside your home or anywhere near you.

2. Protect yourself from infection.
    o   Wash your hands regularly and often. Try to keep your hands away from your face. Remember: most germs spread from hands to mouth.
    o   Get a flu shot each year and consider getting a pneumonia vaccination.
    o   Avoid crowds, especially in winter: more people have colds and flu then.
    o   Try to get plenty of sleep.
    o   Get regular exercise.
    o   Eat a healthy, moderate diet.
    o   Learn postural drainage and percussion. These techniques help you to cough up the extra mucus that would trap germs inside your lungs.

3. Take your medications *exactly* as prescribed. Don't skip doses.

4. Make a follow-up appointment as directed.

Finally, you should call your doctor immediately if you experience any of the following symptoms:

-   Shortness of breath, wheezing, or coughing
-   Tightness in your chest that doesn't go away with rest or medication
-   Irregular heartbeat
-   Increased mucus
-   Yellow, green, bloody, or smelly mucus
-   Fever or chills
-   Swollen ankles

TEXT B   EDUCATION: Pupil Enrollment

In order to enroll a child in a public school system in Virginia, state law requires parents or legal guardians to submit the following information.

-   *Birth Certificate*

An official certified copy of the child's birth record must be provided. (A photocopy of the child's birth certificate will not meet this requirement.) At the time of enrollment, the child must be five years of age or reach his/her fifth birthday on or before September 30th of the school year. If a certified copy of the child's birth record cannot be obtained, the person enrolling the child must submit a sworn statement setting forth the child's age and explaining the inability to present a certified copy of the birth record.

- *Street Address*

Documentation of the street address or route number of the child's residence must be provided.

- *School Entrance Health Form*

A School Entrance Health Form MCH 213 D, completed by a licensed physician, licensed nurse practitioner, or licensed physician's assistant regarding the child, must be presented at the time of enrollment. The three-part form includes Part 1 - Health Information Form, Part II - Comprehensive Physical Examination Report, and Part III – Certification of Immunization.

- *Immunizations*

Documentation (Part III of the School Entrance Health Form MCH 213 D) indicating that the child has received the required immunizations must be provided.

- *Social Security Number*

The child's federal social security number must be provided upon enrollment or within 90 days thereafter. However, a child may not be excluded from school if a social security number is not provided.

- *Expulsion Statement*

When a student is registered, the parent must provide a sworn statement about whether the child has been expelled. The statement must indicate whether the child has been expelled from attending a private school or another public school in Virginia or a school in another state for an offense involving weapons, alcohol or drugs, or for willful infliction of injury to another person.

- *Enrollment of Homeless Students*

Project HOPE ensures the enrollment, attendance, and the success of homeless children and youth in school through public awareness efforts across the commonwealth and sub grants to local school divisions.

TEXT C   **HUMAN SERVICES: Refugee Resettlement**

(Information adapted from the U.S. Office of Refugee Resettlement)

This resettlement program is carried out under the authority of Title IV, Chapter 2, of the Immigration and Naturalization Act, which came out of the Refugee Act of 1980. The goal is to achieve successful social integration for each refugee family as soon as possible after they arrive in the U.S. The first emphasis is on jobs, to help you attain some sort of economic self-sufficiency. Refugees are men, women, and children from all parts of the world who are forced to flee their homelands because of wars, armed conflicts, and gross violations of human rights.

Many refugees have faced persecution because of race, religion, or political opinions, and this can create a lot of stress as you settle into your new life. This program is designed to support you in many different ways while you adjust to your new life here in the United States.

TEXT D   **HUMAN SERVICES: Area Agencies on Aging**

(From Mid Florida Area Agency on Aging at http://www.mfaaa.org/.)

Area Agencies on Aging (AAAs) were established under the Older Americans Act (OAA) in 1973 to respond to the needs of Americans aged 60 and over in every local community. This state has seventeen AAAs, covering all 87 counties. This state's 17 Area Agencies on Aging strive to meet the needs of the rapidly-growing number of older residents of the state. Our Area Agencies:

- Assess current needs of older residents;
- Assess available services, programs, and institutions;
- Develop plans to help address service gaps via the Senior Living Program;
- Assure access to services, programs, and institutions;
- Advocate for the needs of older residents;
- Finance and administer contracts to direct providers of services;
- Provide a central leadership role for older residents; and
- Provide information and assistance services for older residents and their caregivers

Area Agencies are funded by approximately 50% in federal funds, state funds, and local contributions. Collaboration with local human service networks leads to more effective use of our resources and services.

TEXT E   **EDUCATION: Goals and Values**

The Eastern Township School Board emphasizes its commitment to the following goals:

- Student-centered programs
- A strong, rigorous core curriculum enriched with a wide range of non-core subjects and activities
- Courses that engage diverse learning styles
- High, obtainable expectations that meet each student's needs and potential
- A safe, healthy school environment
- An orderly atmosphere that promotes respect for all
- Programs that incorporate awareness of other cultures, languages and world views
- Appropriate space, lighting and ventilation for all programs and activities
- Accountability of schools, teachers, administrators, programs students and curricula

through ongoing, measurable assessment
- Ongoing, timely communication with families about their children's education, progress and programs
- Engagement with the broader community

TEXT F   HEALTHCARE: PTSD

Post Traumatic Stress Disorder (PTSD)

Posttraumatic Stress Disorder (PTSD) is an anxiety disorder caused by experiencing a traumatic event or events. A traumatic event is something frightening and often horrific that the individual has witnessed or experienced. The event may feel life threatening and terrify the individual or make that person feel that s/he has no control over what is happening.

The types of events that have often triggered PTSD include:

- Childhood sexual or physical abuse
- Combat or other wartime experiences
- Sexual or physical assault
- Major accidents, including car accidents
- Terrorist attacks
- Natural disasters, including earthquakes, hurricanes and floods

It is normal to feel upset and angry after such events. However, if those feelings stay or get worse, they may lead to a diagnosis of PTSD. Symptoms of PTSD may be so painful, terrifying, bewildering and disruptive that they interfere with daily activities. They may begin soon after the event, months later, or even years or decades later. Broadly speaking there are four categories of symptoms: reliving the event (nightmares and flashbacks); avoidance; going numb; and hyper-arousal.

TEXT G   HUMAN SERVICES: Child Protective Services (CPS)

Child Protection Services (CPS) is a program offered by Horizon County Department of Social Services. CPS is concerned with the care, safety, and protection of abused or neglected children. Horizon County CPS offers five major services: an Abuse Hotline, protective investigations, in-home services, out-of-home services, and adoptions. During Fiscal Year 2010, 225,000 calls were made to the Abuse Hotline, of which 140,000 were serious enough to be investigated. During the same time period, the program identified 65,000 victims of abuse and neglect, provided protective supervision to 23,000 families, provided out-of-home services to 26,000 children, and placed 900 children in adoptive homes.

Our review of the program determined that:
- The program provides beneficial services that help to preserve families and should be continued.

- The program has not yet met its legislative goals for keeping all Horizon County children safe from abuse and neglect and for finding children permanent homes and must take additional steps to implement more effective child protection strategies.
- The department must enhance the transition from foster care and related services to community-based care lead agencies.

TEXT H   **EDUCATION: School Philosophy**

The Eastern Township School Board believes that the continuation of our democracy depends first and foremost on developing an educated and informed citizenry. The Board also believes that its schools should make every effort to maximize the strengths, assets and potential of all students, so that they may become well-rounded and productive citizens with a strong sense of confidence and civic responsibility. The Eastern Township School Board has set as its goal to endow all students with a broad knowledge base that incorporates effective communication skills, rational thought systems and appropriate expressions of creativity.

Eastern Township Public Schools aims to prioritize an education process that supports the development of an inquiring mind, respect for learning, ethical behavior, and a keen grasp of the rights and responsibilities of citizenship. The schools also seek to inculcate an understanding and appreciation of our national culture and other cultures while nurturing the vision that each and every individual has merit.

OBJECTIVE 2.2
Analyze and practice basic interpreter skills.

2.2 (a) Demonstrate professional introductions, positioning and use of direct speech.
2.2 (b) Develop message analysis, note-taking and memory skills sufficient to interpret two to three sentences accurately without asking for repetition.
2.2 (c) Practice basic interpreting skills in simple role plays.

Exercise 2-i   **Introductions**

Refer to the basic model below for a professional introduction. First, add anything in the blank lines below it that you feel is important and appropriate. Then *practice your introduction with a partner*. Each person should perform the introduction at least once in both languages.

Try to smile and be friendly during your introduction, to build rapport.

Introduction (when speaking to the client, use the language of the client)

▶ Name and agency
▶ Everything said will be interpreted, exactly as it is said.
▶ Everything will be kept confidential.
▶ Please speak directly to each other, not to me.
▶ Please speak slowly and pause often.

Insert here any additional items that the interpreter wishes to add to this introduction (e.g., "Please use first person," "Please use simple language and avoid jargon," or "Please don't say anything you don't wish me to interpret, since I am obligated to interpret everything.") If you are unsure about something you want to add, ask your instructor.

_____
_____
_____
_____

Exercise 2-j   **Memory Skills**

The instructor will display a list of words displayed on a screen. You will have 60 seconds to examine the objects, pictures or words before the instructor covers up the display. Now write down the items (or words) you remember seeing:

_____
_____
_____
_____

The instructor will now display a list of words. After the list is covered up, again, write down as many items from the second list as you can:

_____

_____

_____

_____

Did you remember more or fewer items the second time? Why?

_____

_____

If you were shown a list of words, which part of the list did you remember most easily? Why?

_____

_____

Exercise 2-k (optional)   Memory skills

Work in pairs. The person playing the interpreter *may not see the text.* Take turns playing the interpreter, remembering to *focus on accuracy and completeness.*

For Text A, one person will read out the first *two* sentences. The interpreter (who does not look at the text) will interpret the two sentences into the target language. Then the person reading aloud will read the first *three* sentences. Let the interpreter interpret all of them. Then read the first *four* sentences, then the first *five.* Keep going in this manner until the interpreter can no longer remember the sentences accurately: test the memory limits of the interpreter. Then switch roles and go through Text B in exactly the same way.

If time permits, switch roles again and execute Text C. Again, the interpreter may not look at the text. However, this time, the person reading aloud should read three sentences at a time. Keep reading three sentences until the text is done. Then switch roles and execute Text C again with the other person playing the interpreter.

TEXT A   HEALTHCARE: Oncology

Mrs. Nguyen, I know you are worried because of your sister's history with breast cancer, and you may want to consider certain types of behavior to help protect yourself. Let me give you an example. You may have heard that physical activity significantly reduces levels of estrogens in postmenopausal women. This may actually be good motivation for some female patients to exercise. You see, postmenopausal women who engage in regular physical activity seem less likely to develop breast cancer, possibly because these women experience significant declines in blood levels of the female hormones. Fat mass also decreases significantly in those who exercise, and greater losses of body fat are associated with larger decreases in certain blood hormone levels that appear to be associated with breast cancer. This may be the reason why exercise could lower breast cancer risk in postmenopausal women. Would you like to hear more?

TEXT B   **EDUCATION: No Child Left Behind**

You must be wondering why your son has to take all these tests when he doesn't really read English yet. It's actually part of a very important law. It all started with former President Bush in 2001. He was so concerned about education that he sent a plan to reform education to Congress. Basically, he asked members of Congress to take a look at how the federal government could help close the achievement gap between disadvantaged or minority students and the rest of the students. The result was the No Child Left Behind Act. This law really emphasizes stronger accountability for schools, and it puts a big emphasis on teaching methods that have been proven to work. It also means that every school has to answer for how well its students perform, so this was a pretty significant academic change and we have to take it seriously. So yes, all children have to take these special tests, even if they don't speak English as a native language. We know you're worried about your son, and many parents don't find this system fair. Believe me, we're struggling hard to make this system fair for all our kids in ESOL. But we can't change the rules, so your child will need to take those tests.

Exercise 2-I   **Note-taking Skills**

You will be divided into same-language pairs. Select a text from Exercise 2-f to read out loud to your partner, *who must close this workbook, listen and take notes on a separate sheet of paper.* After you have finished reading each part of the text out loud, your partner will then interpret what you have said into the target language, and you will give feedback about how accurate your partner's rendition was

When you have completed the exercise, exchange roles and perform the same exercise with a different text from Exercise 2-f. Continue until the instructor asks you to stop and answer the following questions:

1. How helpful were your notes?

_____

_____

2. What kinds of things did you note down?

_____

_____

3. Did you notice any errors you made while note-taking (such as taking too many notes or writing illegibly)? What were your errors?

_____

_____

4. What areas of your note-taking would you like to improve most?

_____

_____

_____

_____

Exercise 2-m: **Consecutive Role Play Practice**

In groups of three who speak the same language, if possible, execute the following role plays in accordance with the directions given by your instructor. Try very hard to interpret at least two to three sentences accurately at a time.

TEXT A EDUCATION/HEALTHCARE: Parent-Teacher Conference

Teacher: Good morning, Mrs. Lopez.

Parent: Buenos días, señorita.

Teacher: The reason we're meeting here this morning is to talk about Luis' academic progress, healthcare history, and his social interactions at home.

Parent: Si, señorita.

Teacher: Mrs. Lopez, how long have you and your family been living in the United States?

Parent: Hace un año que nos vinimos acá al norte, por eso no conocemos muchas cosas de este país.

Teacher: Does your family like this change?

Parent: No, señorita, pero vivimos mejor aquí que en nuestro país. Tenemos por lo menos trabajo y comida, y así no nos morimos de hambre.

Teacher: Mrs. Lopez, Luis did not pass the reading test. He does not know his ABCs, and he does not recognize them or their sounds. He is behind the rest of the class academically. I am very concerned.

Parent: ¿Cómo se comporta mi Luis en la clase, señorita?

Teacher: That's another concern of mine, Mrs. Lopez. He's not making friends and he refuses to talk to his classmates. He only answers yes or no questions, and when he's at the playground he plays by himself.

Teacher: Good morning, Mrs. Lopez.

Parent: Good morning, Miss.

Teacher: The reason we're meeting here this morning is to talk about Luis' academic progress, healthcare history, and his social interactions at home.

Parent: Yes, Miss.

Teacher: Mrs. Lopez, how long have you and your family been living in the United States?

Parent: We came north a year ago. That's why we don't know much about this country.

Teacher: Does your family like this change?

Parent: No, Miss, but we live better here than in our country. At least we have work and food, so we won't die of hunger.

Teacher: Mrs. Lopez, Luis did not pass the reading test. He does not know his ABCs, and he does not recognize them or their sounds. He is behind the rest of the class academically. I am very concerned.

Parent: How does my Luis behave in class, Miss?

Teacher: That's another concern of mine, Mrs. Lopez. He's not making friends and he refuses to talk to his classmates. He only answers yes or no questions, and when he's at the playground he plays by himself.

Parent: ¡Dios mío!

Teacher: Mrs. Lopez, could you please tell me about Luis' health problems?

Parent: Luis tiene muchos problemas de salud.

Teacher: What kind of health problems does he have?

Parent: Pues, le voy a contar la historia de Luis desde que nació. Luis nació a los siete meses.

Teacher: Was he born premature?

Parent: No sé qué es eso, pero casi se me muere mi cipote. Estuvo en el hospital dos meses porque no podía respirar.

Teacher: Did you know why he couldn't breathe?

Parent: Sí, sí, señorita, pues, el doctor nos dijo que sus pulmones no se habían desarrollado bien todavía, y por eso se quedó en el hospital.

Teacher: Good. Now, Mrs. Lopez, I want to talk about how Luis interacts with his siblings at home.

Parent: Pues, no muy bien que digamos. Se pasa sentado en un hueco, y no hay quien lo saque de allí.

Teacher: Why do you think he does that, Mrs. Lopez?

Parent: Oh my goodness!

Teacher: Mrs. Lopez, could you please tell me about Luis' health problems?

Parent: Luis has a lot of health problems.

Teacher: What kind of health problems does he have?

Parent: Well, I'll tell you about Luis when he was born. Luis was born at seven months.

Teacher: Was he born premature?

Parent: I don't know what that is, but my son almost died on me. He was in the hospital for two months because he couldn't breathe.

Teacher: Did you know why he couldn't breathe?

Parent: Yes, yes, well, the doctor told us that his lungs had not developed well yet, and that's why he stayed in the hospital.

Teacher: Good. Now, Mrs. Lopez, I want to talk about how Luis interacts with his siblings at home.

Parent: Well, not very well, really. He spends the day sitting in a corner, and nobody can get him out of it.

Teacher: Why do you think he does that, Mrs. Lopez?

Parent:	No sé señorita, pero hemos tratado de llevarle al doctor, y es muy caro. Mi marido y yo trabajamos, y el pisto que ganamos no nos alcanza para nada. No tenemos seguro, y por eso no sabemos cuál es el problema. Sus hermanos no quieren jugar con él porque llora mucho y no quiere hablar.	**Parent**:	I don't know, Miss. We've tried to take him to the doctor, but it's very expensive. My husband and I work, but the money we earn isn't nearly enough. We don't have insurance, and that's why we don't know what the problem is. His brothers and sisters don't want to play with him because he cries a lot and doesn't want to talk.
Teacher:	I've noticed some of that behavior here in school with his classmates. It seems difficult for him to make friends.	**Teacher**:	I've noticed some of that behavior here in school with his classmates. It seems difficult for him to make friends.
Parent:	¿Qué hago? Estoy muy preocupada, pero tengo que trabajar, y no me puedo quedar en la casa para cuidarlo, porque si lo hago no tenemos para comer.	**Parent**:	What can I do? I'm very worried but I have to work, so I can't stay home to take care of him because if I do then we won't have food on the table.
Teacher:	I'll see what I can do for him. I'm sure we can find some help here in school.	**Teacher**:	I'll see what I can do for him. I'm sure we can find some help here in school.
Parent:	Qué Dios me la bendiga, señorita.	**Parent**:	God bless you, Miss.
Teacher:	Thank you. How are your other children doing in school?	**Teacher**:	Thank you. How are your other children doing in school?
Parent:	Mis otros chamacos están bien. Sólo es mi Luis el que tiene problemas, y yo sufro mucho.	**Parent**:	My other children are fine. It's just my Luis that has problems, and it's very hard for me.
Teacher:	Is Luis your youngest son?	**Teacher**:	Is Luis your youngest son?
Parent:	Sí, él es el último de mis patojos.	**Parent**:	Yes, he is the last of my kids.
Teacher:	Mrs. Lopez, I am going to talk to the teacher that helps students after school about helping Luis with his homework.	**Teacher**:	Mrs. Lopez, I am going to talk to the teacher that helps students after school about helping Luis with his homework.
Parent:	Gracias, señorita.	**Parent**:	Thank you, Miss.

Teacher:	I'll talk to my colleagues about evaluating Luis to determine what kind of help he needs, and also to refer him to a free clinic.		**Teacher**:	I'll talk to my colleagues about evaluating Luis to determine what kind of help he needs, and also to refer him to a free clinic.
Parent:	OK.		**Parent**:	OK.
Teacher:	Do you have any other questions, Mrs. Lopez?		**Teacher**:	Do you have any other questions, Mrs. Lopez?
Parent:	Sí, quiero preguntarle, ¿qué debemos hacer en la casa para ayudar a Luis?		**Parent**:	Yes, I wanted to ask you what we should do at home to help Luis.
Teacher:	You and your family have to be very patient with him, and give him lots of love. This is a long process, and all of us are going to work together to help Luis become a healthy and happy boy.		**Teacher**:	You and your family have to be very patient with him, and give him lots of love. This is a long process, and all of us are going to work together to help Luis become a healthy and happy boy.
Parent:	Gracias, señorita, ahora si me voy contenta sabiendo que mi Luis va a estar mejor.		**Parent**:	Thank you, Miss. Now I'm happy, knowing that my Luis will get better.
Teacher:	Yes, don't worry, he will be OK. As soon as I talk to my colleagues, I will contact you by phone.		**Teacher**:	Yes, don't worry, he will be OK. As soon as I talk to my colleagues, I will contact you by phone.
Parent:	Gracias. Esperaré su llamada. No sé cómo la voy a pagar.		**Parent**:	Thank you. I'll wait for your call. I don't know how to thank you.
Teacher:	It's my pleasure, Mrs. Lopez.		**Teacher**:	It's my pleasure, Mrs. Lopez.
Parent:	Gracias, señorita.		**Parent**:	Thank you, Miss.
Teacher:	Good-bye.		**Teacher**:	Good-bye.
Parent:	Adiós.		**Parent**:	Good-bye.

Exercise 2-n **Intake Role Plays**

Role plays should reflect the service area of the participants in the group, e.g., healthcare interpreters should practice healthcare role plays. Freelance/contract interpreters may practice role plays from a variety of services.

After selecting a service area, quickly establish a common situation in that profession. In groups of three set up the role play for basic intake. Let the interpreter make an introduction. Then the person playing the provider should ask five or six questions, while the client/patient makes up answers. Choose at least two to three role plays from the list below. Take turns, and allow everyone to play the interpreter.

Examples:

Situation 1: Human and Social Services   *An immigration clinic*
A client gets upset because the immigration counselor says he or she has missed the deadline to apply for a renewal of the Temporary Protected Status and work permit.

Situation 2: Education   *A Special Education diagnostic center ("Child Find")*
A parent insists that his or her child does not need "special education" and that the only problem with the child is a language barrier.

Situation 3: Healthcare   *A free clinic*
A woman has just learned she has a Sexually Transmitted Disease (STD) named gonorrhea that she must have received from her husband and she is very upset.

Situation 4   *Social services*
The client is told that she is not eligible for Social Service benefits (food stamps and temporary cash assistance) because she is the stepmother and not the mother of the children in that refugee family. She is confused and asks questions.

Situation 5: Healthcare   *Hospital*
A nurse notices that a female patient presenting with abdominal pains also has unusual bruises and lacerations. Concerned about possible domestic violence that could also explain the abdominal pain, the nurse asks a few questions about when the patient got the bruises, how they happened, where the incident occurred, if the bruises still hurt, etc.

Situation 6: Education   *A Parent-Teacher Conference*
An elementary teacher welcomes a parent warmly to a parent-teacher conference and they discuss the child's latest grades and progress in math and reading.

Situation 7: Healthcare   *A pediatric department*
Prior to administering a DTaP vaccine (for diphtheria, tetanus and pertussis) a nurse asks a parent a few questions e.g., is the child allergic to any medications, is the child sick, how sick, has the child ever had a seizure or collapsed after taking DTaP before, etc.

UNIT 3   CULTURE AND MEDIATION

OBJECTIVE 3.1
Demonstrate effective mediation skills.

3.1 (a) List and practice the steps for mediation.
3.1 (b) Practice strategic mediation.
3.1 (c) Define and compare interpreter roles.

Exercise 3-a   Steps for Mediation

Without looking at your manual, unscramble the steps for mediation and put them in the correct order in the lines below.

Interpret what you said for the other party; address one party briefly; interpret what was just said; return to basic interpreting; identify yourself as the interpreter.

1. _____
2. _____
3. _____
4. _____
5. _____

Exercise 3-b (optional)   What to Remember!

List at least four of the things that many interpreters forget to do when they mediate.

_____
_____
_____
_____

Exercise 3-c   Practicing Mediation

Following the directions of your instructor, in pairs or groups of three practice the following examples of strategic mediation out loud. Sight translate the text for the client into your target languages. The goal is simply to practice saying out loud some examples of mediation that you might say in real life.

1. CLARIFICATION:
   Situation: The interpreter does not understand something said by the provider or client.

Script:

(to provider) "Excuse me, as the interpreter I wanted to ask the client what he means by *cochinillas.*"

(to client) "Excuse me, as the interpreter I wanted to ask what you mean by *cochinillas.*"

2. CHECKING FOR UNDERSTANDING:

Situation: The client appears not to understand what the provider says, but the provider seems unaware of this problem.

Script:

(to provider) "Excuse me, as the interpreter I sense a break in communication that might be caused by a misunderstanding about what consent forms are."

(to client) "I just informed the provider that I sensed a communication problem that might be caused by a misunderstanding about what consent forms are."

3. HIGH REGISTER

Situation: The provider is using PhD English with a client who has little education.

Script:

(to provider) "Excuse me, as the interpreter I'm not sure that what I am interpreting is clear. If you would like to rephrase in simpler language, I may be able to interpret it more clearly."

(to client) "Excuse me, as the interpreter I just informed the provider that what I am interpreting may not be clear. I suggested she rephrase in simpler language, so that I can interpret it more clearly."[1]

4. CULTURAL-LINGUISTIC BARRIER

Situation: The provider is using the client's last name as their first name and vice versa.

Script:

(to provider) "Excuse me, as the interpreter I'm concerned there may be an inaccurate record for this client's name due to a different naming system in the client's country. You may wish to ask the client about this."

(to client) "Excuse me, as the interpreter I just informed the provider that there may be an inaccurate record for your name due to the different naming system in our country. I suggested she might want to ask you about this."

5. BASIC CULTURAL BARRIER

Situation: During a parent-teacher interview, a child's father has no idea what is going on and you suspect the problem is that he has never even heard of, much less seen, a report card.

Script:

(to provider) "Excuse me, as the interpreter I'm concerned there may be a misunderstanding about the purpose of a report card."

(to client) "Excuse me, as the interpreter I told the teacher I'm concerned there may be a misunderstanding about the purpose of a report card."

---

[1] Notice how this type of mediation does not insult the client's education or literacy level. It is very important that whatever you say to the provider be something that you can also say to the client without sounding condescending or offensive.

6. COMPLEX CULTURAL BARRIER
   Situation: During a child protective services investigation, a parent shuts down and the interpreter senses a serious cultural barrier.
   Script:
   (to client) "Excuse me, as the interpreter I'm concerned there may be a cultural misunderstanding related to family roles between husband and wife. Service providers often find it helpful to hear cultural information. Is there anything you'd like to share with the provider?"
   (to provider): "Excuse me, as the interpreter I'm concerned there may be a cultural misunderstanding related to gender roles. I asked the client if there anything he'd like to share with you about this topic."
   (Note: it is often preferable to address the provider first unless the interpreter senses an important cultural barrier that is causing tension. In that case, addressing the client first may help to defuse the tension.)

7. SERVICE DELIVERY BARRIER
   Situation: The service provider, during intake, is asking many questions which appear intrusive and culturally upsetting, e.g., past sexual behavior and partners. The interpreter watches the session derail and fears that the patient will not take the necessary tests or adhere to a treatment plan.
   Script:
   (to provider) "Excuse me, as the interpreter, I'm concerned that some of these questions may appear upsetting or culturally intrusive to many people from the patient's culture."
   (to patient) "Excuse me, as the interpreter, I shared with the provider that some of these question may appear upsetting or culturally intrusive to many people from or culture."

8. CLIENT SPEAKS TO INTERPRETER
   Situation: The client tells the interpreter, during the session, "I'm not sure about this. Do you think the provider is giving me good information?"
   Script:
   No script. Simply interpret the comment and let the provider answer the question.

9. PROVIDER SPEAKS TO INTERPRETER
   Situation: The provider asks the interpreter, "Do you think my client understands?"
   Script:
   First, interpret the question. Then remind the provider:
   (to provider) "Excuse me, as the interpreter I want to remind you that I must interpret everything you say and that I'm not permitted to answer questions during a session."
   (to client) "Excuse me, as the interpreter I just reminded the provider that I must interpret everything he says and can't answer questions during the session."

Exercise 3-d   **Mediation Scripts**

One of the greatest challenges when performing mediation is knowing exactly what to say when a communication barrier arises. To prepare for this, you should get in the habit of having your own mental scripts for common or typical situations that arise. You should mentally prepare to say things that sound natural for you. For all the examples below, do not write anything from this manual. Instead, write down what *you* might say in real life.

"WHAT SHOULD I SAY?"

For each situation below, write down in the blank lines provided what you think the interpreter should say. After the group has discussed your answers, take turns practicing what you have written with your partner. (Don't worry about positioning: focus only on practicing what you say when you perform the mediation.)

1. The provider uses a term you do not know. *When you mediate, what will you say to each person?*

_____
_____
_____
_____

2. The client seems completely lost because the provider is speaking at a very high register, but you are not allowed to simplify the provider's message. The provider is giving very important instructions and you are obligated to facilitate communication. *When you mediate, what will you say to each person?*

_____
_____
_____
_____

3. While you are interpreting, the provider uses a term like "IEP" (in education), "financial qualification form" (in human services) or "advance directive" (in healthcare). You are not aware of a direct, equivalent term in the target language. In addition, the concept does not appear to exist in the culture of the client, and the client has a low level of literacy. NOTE: DO <u>NOT</u> EXPLAIN THE TERM TO THE CLIENT YOURSELF. *When you mediate, what will you say to each person?*

_____
_____
_____
_____

4. A parent arrives at school to meet a teacher. You find out this is the parent's first parent-teacher meeting. The client comes from a rural area of a culture where the system of education is so different that the parent does not even understand what a report card is. When the meeting begins, the teacher does not notice the problem, but the client quickly grows confused about the child's report card. *When you mediate, what will you say to each person?*

_____

_____

_____

_____

5. During a mental health intake, the provider asks many personal questions. As the interpreter, you know that in the culture of the client, such questions appear intrusive and sometimes bizarre. (For undocumented immigrants, there might also be the fear of being reported to immigration.) Finally the client bursts out in anger to you, "Why is she asking me all these questions? Does she ask everybody? Or is it because I'm an immigrant?" *When you mediate, what will you say to each person?* (Note: in real life you might not need to mediate because a sensitive provider will know what to do if you simply interpret the client's exclamation. However, for purposes of this role play, assume that you need to mediate.)

_____

_____

_____

_____

Exercise 3-e   **Practice the Steps for Mediation**

Execute the following role plays according to the directions of your instructor.

Role Play A   **ANY SECTOR: Request to Speak Slowly**

In groups of three, let one person play a client who is upset about a problem and speaks so quickly that the interpreter must gently interrupt the client. When interrupting the session, remember to:

- Lean or step forward.

- Make eye contact with both parties (you have been avoiding eye contact while interpreting).

- Say something clear and simple, e.g., "Excuse me, as the interpreter, I need to ask the client to speak more slowly and pause to allow me time to interpret." Then state in the other language: "Excuse me, as the interpreter could I ask you to speak more slowly and pause to allow me time to interpret? Thank you."

Role Play B HEALTHCARE: Traditional Medicine

Number of participants: 3
Roles: Physician, patient, interpreter
Setting: Free clinic

A patient is being interviewed by a doctor about symptoms of abdominal pain. The doctor asks "What have you been taking for the pain?" The patient uses a word that refers to a form of traditional medicine. (Try to use something you know from your own culture, e.g., *Fan ji* in China—a mixture of herbs.)

When mediating, keep the process simple. Example: To the provider say, "Excuse me, as the interpreter I'd like to clarify the meaning of *fan ji* with the patient." Interpret your mediation for the patient, and the patient can continue by saying something like this:

Patient: Oh, it's a mixture of Chinese herbs. You know, Chinese medicine. I use the *fan ji* my aunt made for me for all these years, but right now it is not helping and maybe it even made the pain worse. (Interpret this text and then switch roles until everyone in your group has played the interpreter.)

Provider:	Ma'am, we're very sorry for your loss. We want to honor your requests to have a funeral according to your religion. Can you please give us some information?
Client:	Gracias. Mi esposo Aashif fue un hombre muy religioso, y siempre seguimos el Quran.
Provider:	I understand, and that's why it is so important that you tell me what you want to do.
Client:	Sharia es nuestra ley religiosa. Primero, debo decirle que no podemos hablar de cremación, eso está prohibido. Lo primero que hacemos en un ritual que llamamos el lavado y envoltura del cuerpo, seguido por una oración llamada Salah.
Provider:	How do you do the bathing and shrouding?
Client:	Su hermano Abdul Kareem tendrá que hacerlo. En nuestra religión, el cuerpo de un hombre tiene que ser lavado solo por otro hombre.
Provider:	Well, we have regulations in this state but I believe you don't have to have a funeral director. The laws for handling a deceased person are very strict. You can't move a body without permission. We need to get permission so his brother can do it.

Provider:	Ma'am, we're very sorry for your loss. We want to honor your requests to have a funeral according to your religion. Can you please give us some information?
Client:	Thank you. My husband Aashif was a very pious man, and we always follow the Quran.
Provider:	I understand, and that's why it is so important that you tell me what you want to do.
Client:	Sharia is our religious law. First, I need to tell you that we won't consider cremation; it's forbidden. The first thing we do is a ritual involving bathing and shrouding the body, followed by Salah, our prayer.
Provider:	How do you do the bathing and shrouding?
Client:	His brother Abdul Kareem will have to do it. In our religion a male's body is to be washed by a male.
Provider:	Well, we have regulations in this state but I believe you don't have to have a funeral director. The laws for handling a deceased person are very strict. You can't move a body without permission. We need to get permission so his brother can do it.

Client: Gracias, estoy muy agradecida. El lavado y la envoltura del cuerpo son muy importantes para nosotros. Debemos mantener el cuerpo de mi esposo cubierto mientras se le lava.

Client: El cuerpo debe lavarse tres, cinco o siete veces – siempre en números nones y al final del baño, usamos aguas de olor.

Provider: Will you be bringing the scented water?

Client: Si, su hermana Abiir va a venir con el agua de olor. El entierro debe de ser lo más pronto posible. Abdul Kareem envolverá el cuerpo. No tenemos visitación ni velatorio. Nos mantenemos en oración y ayuno y cuando enterremos a mi esposo, su cara debe de estar en dirección a la Mecca.

Provider: [Speaks to the _**INTERPRETER**_, not the client] Do you think you could talk to me after the session to explain Muslim funerals? I'm a little confused.

What should the interpreter do?

Client: Thank you, I'm grateful. Washing and wrapping the body is also very important for us. We need to keep my husband's body covered while washing.

Client: The body has to be washed three, five or seven times-always an odd number of times and in the final washing, we use scented water.

Provider: Will you be bringing the scented water?

Client: Yes, her sister Abiir will come with this special water. The burial has to be done as soon as we can. Abdul Kareem will do the enshrouding of the body. We do not have visitation. We stay in prayer and fasting and when we bury my husband, his head has to face towards Mecca.

Provider: [Speaks to the _**INTERPRETER**_, not the client] Do you think you could talk to me after the session to explain Muslim funerals? I'm a little confused.

What should the interpreter do?

Exercise 3-f   **Interpreter Roles**

If the interpreter in the following situations takes the decision to mediate, what role would the interpreter adopt: conduit, clarifier, cultural mediator or advocate? Write your answer down in the blanks provided.

1. The community health nurse summarizes a document, and the interpreter accurately interprets her summary. _____

2. The counselor uses the term PTSD, and the interpreter does not know what PTSD means and asks about it. _____

3. The Hmong interpreter is supposed to interpret "radiation treatment" but finds no equivalent in Hmong for such a term, or even a clear way to express the concept.

    _____

4. The Muslim African client keeps her eyes completely averted from the male provider and won't answer. The interpreter realizes that the client may, for religious or cultural reasons, feel uncomfortable with a male provider.

    _____

5. An administrative aide asks the interpreter to place a phone call to a client to confirm an appointment. The interpreter is alone while making the call.

    _____

6. The doctor leaves the room when the patient has not understood how to take the prescribed medication. The interpreter is concerned that the patient's health could suffer greatly as a result and with the patient's permission finds a nurse and shares her concern. _____

7. The substance abuse therapist explains the rules of the homeless shelter to the client, including the fact that a positive result on a drug test will result in automatic expulsion. The client blows up and curses at the therapist. The interpreter interprets everything, including the curses. _____

8. The income assistance specialist asks the interpreter to help the client fill out a form and leaves the interpreter alone with the client. It is part of the interpreter's primary job to help clients with forms. _____

Develop and practice cultural mediation strategies.

3.2 (a) Define culture and cultural competence.
3.2 (b) Apply ethical decision-making to a communication barrier.
3.2 (c) Practice basic interpreting skills in simple role plays.
3.2 (d) Show awareness of stereotypes and bias.

Exercise 3-g: **Components of Culture**

Culture can be defined in many ways… Here is one way to consider culture:

The ways of being and understanding that define a social group, including shared knowledge, attitudes, beliefs, values, traditions, art, science, education and worldview.

What does culture include? Fill in the figures below with examples of physical, family, personal and social aspects of culture.

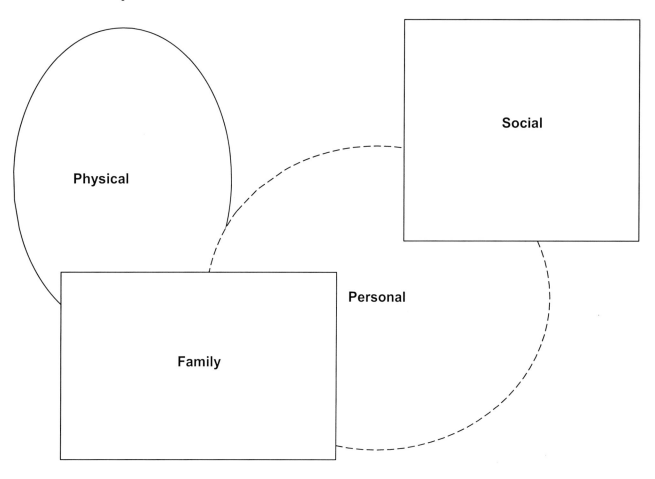

Exercise 3-h   Cultural Competence

In small groups, read the definitions of cultural competence presented on p. 198 of your manual. Decide which definition your group prefers, and why.

_____

_____

_____

_____

Exercise 3-i   Decision-making

The decision to mediate should never be taken lightly. As you discuss your answers to the following questions in small groups, consider the ethical decision-making guidelines from the California Healthcare Interpreting Association (CHIA). They are discussed on pp. 204-206 of your manual.

	WHAT WOULD YOU DO? **Will you mediate or simply continue to interpret?** **If you choose to mediate, say why (or why not).**
Head Start	The family comes in to meet a teacher who recommends that their child be tested to see whether the child needs Special Education Services. The family grows angry because they believe the child's problem is only a language barrier and their child needs no Special Education services.
Homeless shelter	A family is about to leave the shelter to start life in an apartment. At the last meeting with the counselor, the father asks you (the interpreter) for a loan of money to help the family through the first month, believing that you will not interpret this, even though in your introduction you made clear that you interpret everything.
Church-based refugee program	A woman who tested negative for tuberculosis (TB) in the refugee camp abroad is telling you privately outside the session that she now has symptoms of TB. You know that it is possible to test negative for TB and still have TB later. The woman begs you to say nothing about the symptoms to anyone.
Domestic violence	A woman is staying in a shelter with her two children, who are causing disruption among other families. She does not stop them. Shelter employees are upset at both the children and mother. The interpreter wonders whether this is happening because the wife has culturally deferred to the father in matters of discipline.
Healthy Families	During an interview where the social worker is asking how the new mother is doing, you sense that her smiling answers are concealing very deep depression or perhaps marital problems because you are

	familiar with the etiquette of the culture. (Healthy Families programs support at-risk pregnant women or families with infants and toddlers.)
Free clinic	A patient with gall-bladder disease is not following the prescribed diet and health plan after seeing a nutritionist. The nurse scolds her for this. Yet you know that the prescribed diet is quite different from the traditional food eaten by this family and that it is impossible for the patient (who has not graduated from primary school) to adopt the prescribed diet without assistance and support.
Infants and Toddlers Program	You are at a hospital visiting a client in labor when you hear a former client in the curtained "room" next door being told by a custodial-staff "interpreter" that she should sign a form to get medication for an infection. But you know from what the nurse was saying that this patient is actually about to sign a consent form for gall bladder surgery, which is major surgery.

Exercise 3-j   **Non-Intrusive Cultural Mediation Role Plays**

Act out the following role plays. Improvise at the end of the role play to give the interpreter a chance to decide whether or not to perform cultural mediation—and, if so, decide what the interpreter should say.

Some of these role plays have a Spanish version and some do not. If there is no Spanish script, then everyone who plays the client or patient must *sight translate the text into the target language.* Doing so is good practice for sight translation skills.

In these role plays, *the person who plays the interpreter cannot see the script.*

TEXT A   **HEALTHCARE: Pediatric Diabetes**

Nurse-practitioner: I want to explain the condition to you. Diabetes is a disease, but it's also a condition and a way of living. I know it may seem a little frightening at first, but let me try to give you some basic information to help demystify the disease. Now, the first thing to keep in mind is that in the child with Type 1 diabetes, which means insulin-dependent diabetes, the pancreas doesn't produce insulin, and insulin is a hormone that's necessary to sustain life.

Parent: You're using words I do not understand. What do you mean insulin? Isn't that the medicine?

Nurse-practitioner: No. Insulin is a hormone produced in the pancreas that regulates the level of glucose in the blood.

Parent: Now you really confused me. What is glucose?

Nurse-practitioner: Glucose means the sugar level in your child's blood. Diabetic children can't control the levels of glucose in their blood; sometimes it's high, and sometimes it's low. Insulin is an artificial hormone that can help him regulate these levels to have a healthy life. You'll understand more as you become more familiar with it.

Parent: So what do I need to learn now?

Nurse-practitioner: Essentially, a person with Type 1 diabetes has to take injections of insulin to stay alive and healthy. And even then insulin isn't a cure. It's just a way of controlling the disease. So when a child with juvenile diabetes isn't feeling well, you may want to look for certain kinds of symptoms—

Parent: You mean, he won't be cured?

Nurse-practitioner: No, I'm sorry.

Parent: (silence)

Nurse-practitioner: I know this isn't easy for you at all, but there are a lot of other children with this disease, and we can refer you to a group where you can talk to other parents of diabetic children. First I need to tell about the symptoms you need to be looking out for: things like...

- Headaches
- Sweating
- Shakiness
- Feeling cold and clammy
- Sharp hunger
- Weakness
- Dizziness
- Fatigue and tiredness
- A rapid pulse rate
- Blurred vision
- Shallow breathing
- The inability to concentrate
- Loss of coordination
- Mental confusion
- Seizures
- Loss of consciousness

Patient: **(to the INTERPRETER, not the doctor)**: I want to find another doctor. This one doesn't understand anything.

Continue this role play by acting out what happens next. Let the interpreter decide whether (and how) to perform cultural mediation, if needed.

Pharmacist: Your prescription is ready.

Patient: Gracias, esta medicina es nueva. ¿Aviane, por qué me habrán dado esta medicina? ¿Puede decirme lo que es esto?

Pharmacist: Aviane is a combination of female hormones that prevent ovulation. It's used to prevent pregnancy.

Patient: ¿Evitar embarazos? No, yo no fui al doctor para esto. Yo fui porque tengo periodos menstruales muy dolorosos e irregulares. ¿Qué tiene que ver esta medicina con mi mes?

Pharmacist: Don't be alarmed. Sometimes doctors prescribe this to help women balance some hormonal imbalance. I'm sure that's why your doctor prescribed it. Do you want to call your doctor to find out why she gave it to you?

Patient: No, voy a estar fuera del país por un largo tiempo y necesito la medicina pero tal vez la pueda conseguir en mi país. Esta medicina me da miedo. ¿Dígame, cuáles son las reacciones?

Pharmacist: Well, there are several, first it is to prevent pregnancy but the dose you have is very small. Some of the reactions are mild nausea, vomiting, bloating, stomach cramps; breast pain, tenderness, or swelling; freckles or darkening of facial skin; increased hair growth, loss of scalp hair; changes in weight or appetite; problems with contact lenses; vaginal itching or discharge;

Patient: ¡Hay es demasiado! …….

Continue the role play by improvising. Let the interpreter decide whether or not to perform cultural mediation.

Pharmacist: Your prescription is ready.

Patient: Thank you, this is a new medication. Aviane, I wonder why I got this medicine. Can you tell me what it is?

Pharmacist: Aviane is a combination of female hormones that prevent ovulation. It's used to prevent pregnancy.

Patient: Prevent pregnancy?! No this is not why I went to the doctor. I went because my menstrual periods are painful and irregular, what does this medication have to do with menses?

Pharmacist: Don't be alarmed. Sometimes doctors prescribe this to help women balance some hormonal imbalance. I'm sure that's why your doctor prescribed it. Do you want to call your doctor to find out why she gave it to you?

Patient: No, I'm going on a long trip and I need the medicine but I wonder if I can get it in my country. This medicine scares me. What are the reactions?

Pharmacist: Well, there are several, first it is to prevent pregnancy but the dose you have is very small. Some of the reactions are mild nausea, vomiting, bloating, stomach cramps; breast pain, tenderness, or swelling; freckles or darkening of facial skin; increased hair growth, loss of scalp hair; changes in weight or appetite; problems with contact lenses; vaginal itching or discharge;

Patient: Oh my, that's too much!…….

Continue the role play by improvising. Let the interpreter decide whether or not to perform cultural mediation.

TEXT C   SOCIAL SERVICES: Food Stamps and Medical Assistance

Number of participants: 3
Roles: Customer, intake worker, interpreter
Setting: Social Services office
Situation: Customer is applying for the supplemental nutrition assistance program (SNAP, still widely known as food stamps) and medical assistance for her U.S.-born children. She has lived in the U.S. for several years. Her husband has a green card. She has no legal documentation in the U.S. *Let the customer make up the answers.* Remember that the interpreter must not look at the script while interpreting.

Questions for the Intake worker (customer will make up the answers):

> Why did you come to this office?
> How long have you been living here?
> Where are you from?
> What type of visa do you have?
> Are you married?
> What is your husband's/wife's immigration status in the U.S.?
> How many children do you have? Were they born in the U.S. or abroad?

Customer gets upset, turns to the interpreter and asks the interpreter (not the provider) in an upset voice: *Why is s/he asking me all these questions!! Does s/he ask everybody these questions or only me? Do I have to answer?*

Now continue acting out the role play naturally and see if the interpreter needs to perform cultural mediation or not.

TEXT D   **HUMAN SERVICES: Domestic Violence**

Number of participants: 3
Roles: Male paralegal, female victim of domestic violence, interpreter
Setting: Office of a domestic violence center

The client is currently staying at the domestic violence shelter with her two children, having escaped an abusive husband who has also sexually assaulted her. She is dressed in the traditional dress of her country, and she does not make eye contact with men. (Cultural note: many women in the client's culture might find it difficult to speak to a male counselor, especially about sensitive subjects.)

This woman's husband has told her she has no legal status in the U.S. He holds her passport and all her papers. But an attorney at the center plans to help the woman to file legal papers to obtain a green card independently of her husband. The paralegal is going to ask her questions to help her.

Note: A woman may play the role of the male paralegal: simply pretend that person is male.

Male paralegal: Good afternoon, Mrs. Abdelrahman. (Interpreter interprets but Mrs. Abdelrahman does not speak or meet the eyes of the counselor)

Male Counselor (gentle, friendly voice): Mrs. Abdelrahman, I'm the counselor who will be helping you find a pro bono attorney for your case. I'm here to ask you a few questions and take down your story before we refer you out to the attorney. That way you may be able to self-petition for a green card independently of your husband.

Interpreter: (interprets the above but Mrs. Abdelrahman still does not speak or meet the eyes of the provider)

Male Counselor: Mrs. Abdelrahman, could you please answer me? We think you have a strong case, and I would really like to help you.

Interpreter: (interprets the above but the client remains silent and distant)

Male Counselor (sounding a little desperate): Could you at least tell me in your own words what's been going on? (when the woman doesn't answer the counselor turns to the *interpreter* and asks:) Can you tell me what's going on here?

Let the interpreter decide what to do and continue acting out the role play to see what happens.

Exercise 3-k (optional)   Cultural Mediation Role Play

Role Play (Generic Service) Setting a Date

A provider in any service is trying to set a date for the client to return for an important follow-up procedure (e.g., surgery, IEP meeting, an appointment with a social worker, etc.). However, the client will not give a straight answer and says many apparently irrelevant things. The provider grows frustrated, and insists on setting a date.

The interpreter is aware of an important religious date in the client's culture that is probably influencing the client's evasiveness. How should the interpreter handle this?

Exercise 3-l   Creating Role Plays

Select from the following situations or adapt one of them to your own employment setting. Create spontaneous role plays based on these situations.

TEXT A   HEALTHCARE: Mental Health, Sexual Assault

Number of participants: 3
Roles: Rape victim, intake therapist, interpreter
Setting: Sexual assault center

A woman from another culture was raped and taken to the hospital. The next day she is taken by her sister to the local sexual assault center for support services, but when the intake therapist asks her what happened, the rape survivor refuses to discuss the event. The interpreter suspects that the client's refusal might be because, in her culture, many raped women feel like social outcasts.

The interpreter notifies the provider that in the culture of the client, the social consequences of rape are often serious and painful, and the provider may wish to explore cultural norms about sexual assault with the client. She then interprets this message for the client, and the provider asks the client how rape is perceived in her country.

TEXT B   HUMAN SERVICES: Subsidized Transportation

Number of participants: 3
Roles: Client services mediator, interpreter, client with disability
Setting: Nonprofit transportation service
Subject: Transportation service

A client with organic brain injury has received a card that allows him to ride a bus for the disabled. But he must make and honor his bus appointments. Twice he has missed those appointments by 10 minutes and after a third time he will lose the bus card. He appears to have no understanding of the importance of promptness in U.S. culture. The exasperated staff member asks the interpreter to explain to the client that time and punctuality are important in America.

The interpreter interprets what is said, then explains that she is not qualified to make explanations but will be happy to interpret whatever the staff member wants to explain. The interpreter then interprets for the client what she has just told the provider.

Exercise 3-m (optional)   Culture and Mediation

Working in pairs:

1. Think of a situation from the past where you were faced with a cultural barrier while interpreting and were not sure what to do about it. Share this story with your partner. Tell your partner what (if anything) you did to address the problem.

2. Let your partner do the same with you.

3. Now decide what each of you would do differently if you faced the same situation today.

UNIT 4 COMMUNITY SERVICES

Exercise 4-a Legal Interpreting Quiz

True or false?

1. Court interpreting is the same as legal interpreting. _____
2. Community interpreters never perform legal interpreting. _____
3. The interpreters on a state Interpreter Registry are all court certified. _____
4. Interpreters in state courts are required to take a test for language proficiency before they get certified. _____
5. About half of interpreters who take a court certification test fail. _____

Community or legal interpreting?

Legal interpreting involves any interpreting for a legal process or proceeding. The fields of community interpreting and court/legal interpreting follow different ethics and standards of practice, and different skills are required. It is therefore important to know the difference.

Are the following examples of *community* interpreting or *legal* interpreting? Or are they a situation that is *related* to legal interpreting, often known as quasi-legal?

Beside each example below (which assumes an interpreter is present), write "C" if you think the situation is community interpreting, "L" if you think the situation is legal interpreting or "Q" if you think the situation is quasi-legal interpreting.

- At a Board hearing, a school Superintendent hears arguments and decides whether or not to expel/suspend a student. _____
- A Child Protective Services investigator interviews a parent about a case of suspected child neglect. _____
- An attorney for a nonprofit legal services organization meets with a woman to discuss her divorce proceedings. _____
- A patient meets with a doctor about a back injury for a Worker's Compensation case. _____
- The interpreter is asked to sight translate a consent form. _____
- A resident from El Salvador meets an immigration counselor to fill out a Temporary Protective Status (TPS) and work permit form. _____
- An ARD (Annual Review and Dismissal) meeting in a school setting. _____
- An elderly resident applies for Supplemental Security Income. _____
- A police officer at the scene of an accident comforts a wife whose husband has just been taken by helicopter to a hospital. Their car was struck head on by a drunk driver. _____
- Same situation as above, but the *husband* was the drunk driver and the police officer asks the wife questions about the accident. _____

- An interview where a U.S. Census Bureau surveyor asks an LEP resident census questions. _____
- A subsidized housing office warns a family that if too many working adults live in their house they will lose their Section-8 housing because they will no longer qualify. _____
- A woman goes to file a Protection Order to prevent her abusive husband from coming near her or their children. _____
- A restaurant worker files a discrimination complaint with a local Office of Human Rights. _____

Exercise 4-b   Legal Interpreting Role Play

Following the instructor's directions, execute the following role play, taking turns.

LEGAL SERVICES: Labor Compensation

Attorney: Good afternoon, and welcome to the Sherrington Employment Center. My name is Steven Goodman, the pro bono lawyer working two days a week at the Employment Center. Are you Mr. Moris Maravilla?

Client: Mucho gusto, Doctor, y gracias por tomar mi caso. Sí, ese mismo soy yo, el mero mero, sí, pero todos me conocen como el Chupacabras. ¿Seria algún problema eso para conseguir mis bolas?

Attorney: I don't think so. Do you have your ID from the Employment Center?

Client: Fíjese que perdí el carné del Centro. Lo perdí en una peda que nos pusimos con el Crazy. Ahora estoy usando una mica que conseguí en Califas.

Attorney: But what is your full, real name?

Client: ¿Como dice? ¡Ah ya! Fíjese que cuando me fui a jalar con el Gringo, yo le di otro nombre, el que aparece en la mica que conseguí en Califas.

Attorney: What name did you give your employer?

Attorney: Good afternoon, and welcome to the Sherrington Employment Center. My name is Steven Goodman, the pro bono lawyer working two days a week at the Employment Center. Are you Mr. Moris Maravilla?

Client: Nice to meet you, Doc, and thanks for taking my case. Yes, that's me, the one and only, yes, but everybody calls me The Boogeyman, heh heh. Will there be a problem for me getting my money?

Attorney: I don't think so. Do you have your ID from the Employment Center?

Client: Well, I lost the card from the Center. I lost it one time when I got crazy drunk. Now I'm using the ID card I got in California.

Attorney: But what is your full, real name?

Client: What? Oh, right! Well, when I went to work with the big boss, I gave him another name, the one that's on the ID card I got in California.

Attorney: What name did you give your employer?

Client:	El nombre que yo le di al Gringo fue el que está en la mica que compré en Los Ángeles, California en 1989, cuando conseguí la mica. Eulalio Pocasangre, sí ese cabalito es el que aparece en la mica.		**Client:**	The name I gave that guy was the one on the ID card that I bought in Los Angeles, California in 1989 -- when I got the card. Eulalio Pocasangre, yes, that's exactly how it is on the card.
Attorney:	Ok, where is the Mica or the identification you provided to the employer?		**Attorney:**	Ok, where is the Mica or the identification you provided to the employer?
Client:	Aquí está, Dr., esta misma. Perdone que ya está toda chuca, pues casi ya ni se puede leer por lo vieja que está. Pero esta es la mera mera que me ha salvado en este pinche país.		**Client:**	Here it is, Doc, this is the one. Sorry it's all dirty—it's so old you can barely read it anymore. But this is the very same one, the one that's saved me in this damn country.
Attorney:	So the name you provided to your employer is the one in this document? It was Eulalio Pocasangre? Is that correct?		**Attorney:**	So the name you provided to your employer is the one in this document? It was Eulalio Pocasangre? Is that correct?
Client:	Correcto, usted cree que ese será un problema para conseguir los chavos que me deben?		**Client:**	Yes. Do you think that will be a problem in getting the cash they owe me?
Attorney:	Do you know how many hours you worked with the employer?		**Attorney:**	Do you know how many hours you worked with the employer?
Client:	Neles, pues fíjese que no me acuerdo para nada. Solo le puedo decir que el jefe siempre nos daba refín a la hora de almuerzo.		**Client:**	No, the thing is I don't remember anything. All I can say is that the boss gave us some really good food at lunchtime.
Attorney:	How much did you ask per hour for your labor?		**Attorney:**	How much did you ask per hour for your labor?
Client:	Como no tengo ninguna especialización, fíjese que solo le pedí ocho bolas por hora. Y creo que le trabajé dos semanas completas. Cree que pueda conseguir de vuelta los chavos?		**Client:**	Since I don't have any special skills, I only asked for eight bucks an hour. And I think I worked two full weeks. Do you think you can get the money back?

Attorney: Yes, Sr. Pocasangre. Please tell him that we are going to make a case now.

Client: Chévere, me llega su modo Dr.

Attorney: But, we need to document as much proof as possible to win this case.

Client: Usted cree, Dr., que esta colilla de uno de los cheques sirva? Pues fíjese que nunca lo cambié, porque siempre me pedían alguna identificación y en ese momento no la encontraba.

Attorney: Yes, Mr. Maravilla, the check stub is good documentation for your case. I'm going to make a copy.

Client: Lo que puedo hacer es buscar más cheques debajo de mi catre y traérselos mañana. Está bien, Dr.

Attorney: How many check stubs do you have?

Client: Yo no sé exactamente cuántos, pero yo los busco y se los presento en la próxima cita.

Attorney: Do you have any witnesses? Somebody else that worked with you that day?

Client: Si, es cierto, hoy que me acuerdo, otros tres cuates trabajaron conmigo durante esas semanas. Pero ya se mudaron para otro estado, y no sé si los puedo ubicar.

Attorney: Mr. Maravilla do you have any relatives in this town?

Attorney: Yes, Sr. Pocasangre. Please tell him that we are going to make a case now.

Client: Great. I like you, Doc.

Attorney: But, we need to document as much proof as possible to win this case.

Client: Doc, do you think that this pay stub from one of the checks will help? You know, I never cashed it, because they kept asking me for some ID, and at the time I couldn't find mine.

Attorney: Yes, Mr. Maravilla, the check stub is good documentation for your case. I_m going to make a copy.

Client: What I can do is look for more checks under my bed, and bring them to you tomorrow. No problem, Doc.

Attorney: How many check stubs do you have?

Client: I'm not sure exactly how many, but I'll look for them and give them to you at the next appointment.

Attorney: Do you have any witnesses? Somebody else that worked with you that day?

Client: Oh, right, now that I think of it there were three other guys working with me those weeks. But they have moved to another state, and I don't know if I can find them.

Attorney: Mr. Maravilla do you have any relatives in this town?

Client:	Sí, Dr., mi jefa vive con mi carnalito en la Ciudad de Baltimore.	**Client**:	Yes, Doc, my wife lives with my brother in Baltimore City.
Attorney:	We need a relative to notarize and prove that you're Mr. Maravilla.	**Attorney**:	We need a relative to notarize and prove that you're Mr. Maravilla.
Client:	Le pediré a mi compadre que me dé un aventón a Baltimore y traer a mi jefecita chula.	**Client**:	I'll ask my buddy to give me a ride to Baltimore to go pick up my pretty little lady.
Attorney:	Good, please make sure you do this tomorrow.	**Attorney**:	Good, please make sure you do this tomorrow.
Client:	Sí, Doctorcito, le traeré a mi jefa la próxima semana.	**Client**:	Sure, Doc, I'll bring my wife next week.
Attorney:	Thank you Mr. Maravilla. I look forward to working with you on this case.	**Attorney**:	Thank you Mr. Maravilla. I look forward to working with you on this case.
Client:	De nada, Doctorcito. Le prometo que le cumpliré con sus pedidos.	**Client**:	You're welcome, Doc. I promise I'll do what you ask.
Attorney:	Good bye and good afternoon, Mr. Maravilla.	**Attorney**:	Good bye and good afternoon, Mr. Maravilla.

Exercise 4-c (optional)   Appropriate or Inappropriate?

In pairs, decide for each situation below whether the request to the interpreter is *appropriate* (A) or *inappropriate* (I) for a professional interpreter. Write "A" or "I" beside each situation and be prepared to justify your answer.

1. A client asks the interpreter to sight translate a piece of correspondence.

2. A client brings a plastic bag full of bills, turn-off notices, junk mail and other correspondence for the interpreter to explain or sight translate.

3. A client asks the interpreter to make two phone calls to schedule appointments with a specialist and a laboratory.

4. A client asks the interpreter to drive him or her to the next appointment.

5. A provider asks the interpreter to sit with a client to sight translate a video for them.

6. During a home visit, a client insists on feeding the interpreter and the social worker a lovely lunch. The social worker accepts. The interpreter hesitates, then accepts.

7. A provider asks the interpreter to translate a consent form.

8. A client asks the interpreter to attend the christening of her baby.

9. A client is ill with terminal cancer and asks that the interpreter visit her in the hospital.

10. A client is selling beautiful enamel paintings depicting scenes of his home country and is hoping the interpreter will purchase one. The interpreter likes it and finds the price is reasonable. She decides to buy one.

11. The interpreter suspects that the child of a client is being abused. After discussions with the case manager for whom the interpreter is interpreting, the interpreter reports the parent to Child Protective Services. Then, the case manager asks the interpreter to inform the parent that the interpreter made the report and why.

12. The client wants the interpreter to be present at each and every court session in a complex divorce case where the abusive husband denies the abuse (when in fact he did commit it). The interpreter is *not* a court interpreter, but the client has had the same interpreter for her counseling sessions at the domestic violence center and will trust no other interpreter for this case.

13. The provider expects the interpreter to sit down with the client to fill out intake forms, financial qualification forms and other paperwork.

14. Social Services expects the interpreter to go from appointment to appointment with the client, within the agency, even though this will involve extended periods of being alone with the client (who wants to know if the interpreter is married, has children, goes to church, etc.).

15. There are no other speakers of the interpreter's language available and the agency would therefore like the interpreter to interpret for someone who comes from a different region and speaks a dialect that the interpreter cannot understand well. When the interpreter tries to decline, the supervisor will not allow it. The interpreter is afraid of losing her job if she does not accept the assignment.

16. A client calls the interpreter at work to say that she (the client) is having chest pains and asks the interpreter for advice. The interpreter is not a nurse. She wants to tell the client to go to ER but she knows that the client has no health insurance. The hospital bill will be at least several hundred dollars to the low thousands depending on what tests are conducted. No one in the interpreter's nonprofit workplace is a clinician. The interpreter calls Ask-A-Nurse, who tells the interpreter to advise the patient to go immediately to ER so the interpreter does so.

17. The interpreter is bilingual. His boss would therefore like the interpreter to solve any and all problems related to immigrant clients.

Exercise 4-d (optional)   Case Studies

The following examples are taken or adapted from real life.

Case Study #1. A bilingual hotline counselor/interpreter who is on call for the sexual assault center where she works is sent on a rape case to the hospital to support a victim from El Salvador. The time is about midnight. The bilingual employee is asked:
- To interpret for the police officer and detective who arrive to investigate the assault.
- To update the bilingual police officer after she arrives by offering a summary of what was said earlier.
- To interpret for the Sexual Assault Forensic Examiner (SAFE) nurse, who conducts a physical rape exam using specialized equipment and a rape exam kit.
- To interpret for the doctor, who prescribes a number of medications (and leaves the interpreter to explain to the rape survivor how to take the medications…)

Then the police decide that this is a false rape report, caused by complex misunderstandings due to language and cultural barriers. The patient's father is called to come and pick her up. On returning to the sexual assault center, the interpreter is asked to report all the details of the incident for:
- The Crisis Intervention Coordinator (her supervisor)
- A weekly staff meeting
- A monthly meeting of hotline counselors who also make hospital visits

---

What ethical principles are involved in this case?

_____

_____

Should this volunteer have agreed to do any/all of the above? What should she have refused to do? If she had been a bilingual employee and not a volunteer, would that make a difference in her ethical requirements as an interpreter?

_____

_____

Whom should she (or could she) have asked for guidance at midnight?

_____

_____

Did any of the requests for information from the interpreter violate confidentiality?

_____

_____

Case Study #2. A social services interpreter speaks fluent French because she is from Québec, but most of the clients she interprets for are from Africa or Haiti. There are many French-speaking countries in Africa, each with a wide range of cultures.

One day the interpreter is asked to interpret for Child Protective Services. They are investigating a charge of neglect: an adolescent girl from Africa cannot speak or care for herself because she is severely developmentally delayed. Her mother is dead; her stepmother refuses to care for her. The school complains that she wears the same clothes for several days in a row and smells. Her father stumbles in responding to these questions, and the interpreter senses a cultural barrier: she knows the general cultural problem but not the details. Yet she feels (through her cultural experience) that the father is both competent and kind and loves the girl, who is present during the interpreted session though she cannot speak. The investigator sees only child neglect.

Which ethical principles are involved here?

_____

_____

What should the interpreter do?

_____

_____

Cultural awareness is an ethical requirement for community interpreters. This bilingual employee is not African or Haitian. How can she develop cultural awareness and competence when serving clients?

_____

P.S. The interpreter, sensing a cultural barrier, interrupted the session and asked if the father wished to share some cultural information about the situation with the investigator. The father was greatly relieved. He told the investigator that in his culture, he could not supervise his daughter's dressing, but the stepmother refused to. The investigator offered to get a home services aide to help the girl dress. The father was even more deeply relieved. He expressed his gratification at being able to speak openly about his culture.

Case Study #3. A nonprofit agency that provides services to immigrants has a client with mental disability caused by organic brain trauma from a car accident. This client speaks limited English; she can barely write. She requires assistance reading her mail, applying for rehabilitative services, leaving a controlling spouse, finding work, corresponding with her son in another state after losing a legal battle for custody that left her with $50,000 in unpaid attorney fees, regaining her driver's license after it was temporarily revoked because of passing out at the wheel, obtaining a pro bono lawyer for bankruptcy proceedings and divorce, applying for QMBY (a form of Medical assistance to supplement Medicare), negotiating the foreclosure of her condo and repossession of her car, applying for low-income housing, coordinating with another case management agency and obtaining Pharmacy Assistance.

The interpreter is one of the two case managers. As a bilingual employee who often interprets, she sees the client once a week. This client is bipolar. She often sits on the floor in a corner of the waiting room or a hallway with her head on her knees. She asks the case manager/interpreter to drive her to appointments. She also wants the interpreter to come with her when she tells her husband to leave her condo and asks her to write letters to her son. She wants to spend several hours in the interpreter's office each week venting about her problems. Then she asks for the interpreter's help obtaining an abortion, which deeply upsets the interpreter, who is personally against abortion although she never speaks of this issue at her workplace. This client begins to cause the interpreter enormous stress and painful feelings.

Which ethical principles are involved?

_____

_____

What should the interpreter do?

_____

_____

Exercise 4-e   **Mediating <u>Outside</u> the Session**

Fill in the blanks below with appropriate things that the interpreter could say. Then pick one of the following two role plays and take turns practicing mediation outside the session. Note: conduct these role plays entirely in English.

When both of you have played the interpreter, if any time is left, execute the other role play.

TEXT A   **HEALTHCARE: Emergency Room Request**

Number of participants: 2
Roles: Supervisor, interpreter
Setting: Hospital prenatal clinic

Supervisor: Julia, I just got a call from ER [Emergency Room]. They desperately need you to go down and interpret for them.

Interpreter: I'm really sorry. I'm comfortable interpreting for prenatal because I know all the terminology and services. But I can't do ER.

Supervisor: Julia, it's an emergency! Somebody's been shot! He's probably going to die, and the whole family's down there.

Interpreter: Then they really need a competent interpreter. It's not just the terminology. I'm an American who knows Spanish, but I've never lived abroad and there are a lot of cultural issues that come up in ER. I don't—

Supervisor: Julia, please, I know this is a bit of a stretch, but can't you make an exception?

Interpreter:

_____
_____
_____
_____

(Give examples of arguments: the interpreter's lack of terminology, the interpreter's lack of cultural expertise, the risk of an adverse health outcome, the risk of offending/hurting the family, the fact that the hospital could be sued for the interpreter's errors, etc. The hospital could use a telephone interpreter to avoid liability until an appropriate in-person interpreter arrives.)

Note: To those who are shocked by the role play above, we must sadly inform you that in many hospitals around the country there are still no staff interpreters or any real understanding of the importance of working only with qualified interpreters in hospital settings.

TEXT B   **EDUCATION: Suspension of a Child**

Number of participants: 2
Roles: Teacher, interpreter
Setting: Elementary school

Interpreter: I'm very sorry, but I can't interpret for this family.

Teacher: But this woman's son has just been suspended, and she's upset. I really need you to stay.

Interpreter: I can't, because I don't speak her dialect.

Teacher: But I was told she speaks [Spanish, Vietnamese—insert appropriate language]

Interpreter: [mediates with the teacher to explain the problem of various dialects and/or regional/indigenous languages. The interpreter then explains why he/she is not qualified to interpret for that family.]

(Example: risk of mistakes, violation of ethics, liability of the school, etc.)

_____

_____

_____

_____

Teacher: Oh. Okay, never mind. The woman brought her young cousin with her, she's a teenager and she speaks English. I'll just use her.

Interpreter: [mediates again to explain the problems of using a family member to interpret]

(Example: cousin is not trained to interpret, is not impartial, may violate confidentiality, the school could use a telephone interpreter instead, etc.)

_____

_____

_____

_____

Activity 4-f   **Strategies for <u>Learning</u> Terminology**

1) What strategies and resources do you think community interpreters should consider if they wish to expand their terminology?

_____

_____

_____

_____

_____
_____
_____
_____
_____
_____

2) What three resources do you plan to purchase or procure first in order to expand your terminology? (Give your top three priorities. For purposes of this exercise, assume that money is no object.)

_____
_____
_____
_____
_____

3) Now look at the terminology section in your manual in the Resources section starting on p.374 and also consider some of the resources that follow (for medical, educational and human and social services interpreters). See if you wish to change, or add to, any of your answers.

_____
_____
_____
_____
_____
_____
_____

Strategies for <u>Retaining</u> Terminology

No one can learn all the thousands of terms needed to interpret scores of community service settings. While your manual has many practical suggestions for resources related to certain areas of terminology, you will have to develop solutions to the challenge of memorizing terminology on your own.

The following are just a few examples of strategies to help you study, memorize and retain terminology. Pick at least three that you intend to practice yourself after leaving this program and write checkmarks beside them.

- Carry a small wire-bound notebook. Write down any new words or medical terms you learn and use them to build a vocabulary list. Study this list regularly.
- Learn two (or more) new medical terms a day in both languages.
- Join a listserv, e.g., the National Council on Interpreting in Healthcare (NCIHC) at www.ncihc.org or the International Medical Interpreters Association at www.imiaweb.org.
- Gather brochures/patient education material/other materials in both languages for new vocabulary.

- Download bilingual materials online on specific diseases or conditions, educational programs or social services programs and so forth (often available in a multitude of languages—a simple search will bring up many). Study them.
- Become a member of ATA's Medical Division and Interpreter Division to receive glossary lists of terms periodically.
- Purchase DVD resources such as Holly Mikkelson's *The Interpreter's Rx* or *Interpretapes* from the University of Arizona and practice with them orally (see Appendix 3 for details).
- Attend a class in Medical Terminology for health or allied health professionals at your local community college. It will deepen your understanding of the terminology and its meaning.
- Carry your personal glossaries everywhere. When you are waiting for an oil change, a dentist appointment or a parent-teacher conference—study your terms.
- Ask other interpreters for their favorite strategies!
- Listen to a medical show on television and interpret simultaneously as you listen.
- Develop specialized glossaries using computer files that you can add to later, e.g., a glossary for prenatal; Special Education programs; Social Security programs like SSDI, SSI, Medicare, etc; STD clinics; and so forth. *Regularly test yourself with these glossaries by arranging the English terms in one column and the other language in the other column.* Block one column (in your weaker language) to see if you know all the terms in your special glossaries.
- Practice Internet word games on the Internet to develop general memory skills.
- Purchase resources to practice consecutive, simultaneous and sight translation vocabulary by interpreting with resources on DVDs such as *The Interpreter's Rx* and *Interpretapes*.

UNIT 5   STANDARDS OF PRACTICE

Exercise 5-a   Respecting Standards

For those of you who had interpreted before coming to this program, think back to your interpreting *before you were trained.* In small groups, execute this exercise about the NCIHC Standards of Practice.

First, look at the NCIHC Standards of Practice in your manual, p. 303-330. Then, under each column, write down by number (e.g., #5), any standard that fits the title. For example, if *before* this training you had always corrected your own mistakes, in the first column (Standards We Always Respected) you could write #5. (The whole group does not have to agree with you.)

But if prior to interpreter training you never replicated the register, style and tone of the speaker, you would write #2 in the third column (Standards We Rarely Respected).

Try to include at least <u>five</u> standards in each column.

Standards We Always Respected	**Standards We Sometimes Respected**	**Standards We Rarely Respected**

Exercise 5-b   Red Light, Green Light, Yellow Light

The instructor will provide every participant with a green, yellow and red circle. In small groups, examine the list below. Each sentence in the list below describes a common interpreting practice (good or bad). In each case, decide if the interpreter should ALWAYS (or almost always) do what the sentence describes. If so, the group should write down Green (or G) beside that practice.

If the practice is something that the interpreter should NEVER (or almost never) do, write Red (or R). If the practice is something the interpreter may *sometimes* do, depending on the circumstances, write Yellow (or Y) and be prepared to justify that answer.

When groups have finished this portion of the exercise, the instructor will read out each bullet below. Everyone in the group will then raise the appropriate colored circle.

1. Interpret everything.
2. Insert your opinion if the client asks you.
3. Add missing information that the provider forgot.
4. Maintain strict confidentiality.
5. Accept money from a client.
6. Ask parties to speak to each other.

7. Let personal beliefs guide your interpreting.
8. Interpret facial expressions and gestures.
9. Change the register (language level) if the provider is using long words, jargon and big sentences.
10. Avoid interrupting the provider.
11. Plan to arrive on time.
12. Tell your colleagues about the details of an interpreted session.
13. Use first person.
14. Instead of helping clients who ask for assistance (such as a ride home), refer them to appropriate social services.
15. Interpret for your family if no other interpreter is offered, e.g., at the hospital.
16. Try to get the client to make the right choice if he is about to lose a service.
17. Convey the spirit, tone and meaning of the message.
18. Talk about what was said at a public event after you performed basic conference interpreting there (e.g., client education seminars, job training, back-to-school-night, health fairs).
19. Violate confidentiality if the client is a danger to himself or others.
20. Interpret obscenities, insults or bigoted statements, no matter how offensive they are.
21. Break confidentiality if required by law.
22. Call yourself a certified interpreter after a 40-hour interpreter training.
23. Use third person when mediating.
24. Send another interpreter in your place if you can't make it.
25. Avoid side conversations at all times while interpreting.
26. Consult a dictionary as needed.
27. Do not interpret literally: interpret the meaning.
28. Stand or sit a little behind the client.
29. Interpret nonverbal noises (unh-unh, mmmm, er, ahem, etc.)
30. Accept small gifts from the client.
31. If another interpreter is already there, insist that you are the right interpreter and that she should leave.
32. Instead of sight translating a legal form, ask the provider to explain it and interpret the explanation.
33. Refuse an assignment that is too difficult.
34. If you find yourself too emotionally involved, withdraw.
35. Always prepare for assignments.
36. Engage in advocacy as needed.
37. Request a break when tired.
38. Drive the client to the next assignment if asked.
39. If you fear a patient does not correctly understand how to take a medication after the appointment, contact a nurse.
40. When performing cultural mediation, make cultural generalizations if needed but avoid stereotypes and judgments.
41. Let the provider leave you alone with the client.
42. Perform sight translation without the provider there if you know the subject of the document well.

Exercise 5-c   Applying Standards

The instructor will display a brief interpreting film vignette. In the lines provided below, write down the numbers of any of the NCIHC standards you felt the interpreter in the vignette *did* respect and any of the standards that you felt she did not respect.

_____

_____

_____

_____

Exercise 5-d   Standards-based Role Plays

Note: In order to have more practice performing sight translation, there are no Spanish scripts for these role plays. All participants who play the role of client or patient will sight translate their text into the target language.

TEXT A   HEALTHCARE: Hospice Patient

NCIHC Standard #12: Promote direct communication.

Number of participants: 3
Roles: Hospice patient, geriatric nurse, interpreter
Setting: A family residence

Nurse: Ask her/him how long s/he's been having pain in his groin.

Interpreter: (makes a waving gesture toward the patient to remind provider to use first person)

Nurse: Oh, that's right. (To patient:) How long have you been having this pain in your groin?

Patient: Since last night. I woke up in the middle of the night screaming with it. Then I couldn't sleep. I take OxyContin for my osteoarthritis, but it's strange, last night the OxyContin had no effect at all.

Nurse: I need to know how bad the pain is and whether it's throbbing or piercing or jabbing or... Interpreter, do you have a way of finding that out for me?

Interpreter: (after interpreting what was said) Excuse me, as the interpreter I wanted to remind you to speak directly to the patient. (Interprets this for the patient.)

Nurse: Oh. (to patient) On a scale of one to ten, how bad would you say the pain was?

Interrupt the role play. (Pretend the session is finished.) The role play will now continue without the patient. Alone with the nurse, the interpreter mediates outside the session to explain the importance of using first person. Reasons to give the nurse:

- First person is more accurate than third person.
- It is faster.
- First person is usually ethically required when interpreting (to ensure accuracy).
- It promotes a stronger provider-patient relationship.
- First person puts less of a strain on the interpreter's memory and concentration.

SPANISH TERMINOLOGY
Osteoarthritis: osteoarthritis; groin: ingle; throbbing pain: latidos de dolor, puntadas, hincadas: piercing pain: dolor que hinca, hincada; jabbing pain: dolor punzante; hospice: residencia para enfermos terminales, hospedería.

TEXT B   **EDUCATION: Pupil Enrollment**

For this role play, the provider will speak quickly. Focus on Standard #4: *The interpreter manages the flow of communication.* The interpreter should be sure to interrupt the provider if s/he goes on too long for the interpreter to perform accurate interpreting.

Parent: I want to register my children in this school. How do I do it? Can I see the principal?

Staff member: Mrs. Ling, you don't need to see the principal. In order to enroll a child in a public school system in Virginia, state law requires us to make sure that the parent or guardian of a child provides this school with certain information. We've prepared a list of that information to help you, so let's go over it together:

Parent: Do I have to be documented?

Staff member: Mrs. Ling, let's review the list and then if you have questions, I can answer them.

Parent: All right.

Staff member: The first thing you need is an official certified copy of the child's birth record. How old is your child?

Parent: Going on five.

Staff member: The child must be five years of age or reach his/her fifth birthday on or before September 30th of the school year.

Parent: Yes, yes, her birthday is August 31.

Staff member: You also need documentation of the street address and a School Entrance Health Form, completed by a licensed physician, licensed nurse practitioner, or licensed physician's assistant.

Parent: I have that.

Staff member: Part III – Certification of Immunization is very important. You child has to be up to date on her immunizations

Parent: Where can I go for that? I believe we have all the shots, but I might be missing one or two.

Staff member: You can go to your pediatrician or you can go to the health department. It opens at 7:30 AM every day. We also need the child's federal social security number—it has to be provided upon enrollment or within 90 days after that. However, a child may not be excluded from school if a social security number isn't provided.

Parent: Oh, uh.... I'm afraid we don't have that.

Staff member: Don't worry; your child can still come to school without it. The last thing we need is a statement indicating whether the child has been expelled from attending a private school or another public school for an offense involving weapons, alcohol or drugs, or for willful infliction of injury to another person.

Parent: But my child is just four years old!

Staff member: Oh yes, that's right. Then you don't need that statement. Do you have any questions?

TEXT C   HUMAN SERVICES: Immigration Counseling

If other groups are working in groups of three and there are only two of you, you may wish to select this immigration counseling role play since it requires only two role-players.

In pairs, have a client ask for the help of the interpreter to read the client's private correspondence, make phone calls and handle an overdue bill. You may conduct this role play in English or, if you speak the same language, in that other language. Read the entire role play and complete good arguments/points (see below) before starting to act it out.

This role play centers on NCIHC Standards of Practice related to maintaining professional role boundaries: standards #16, #17 and #18. The idea is to limit your involvement with clients as much as possible because once they know you as the interpreter, especially if you are a bilingual employee, they may seek you out and try to have you perform other services for them that are not in your job description.

Number of participants: 2
Roles: Client, interpreter
Setting: Area Agency on Aging senior center (or another service if desired)

Client: Do you have a moment?

Interpreter: How can I help you?

Client: I received some mail that I don't understand. Do you think you could look at it for me? (she hands over a letter)

Interpreter: (glances down) This looks like a bill from your gas and electric company. It looks like it's overdue, because they're threatening to cut off your energy in two weeks.

Client: Oh, no! Could you please call them for me? And I have these other letters, they may be important too!

Interpreter: (gently) Unfortunately, I'm not allowed to do that. But I'd be happy to refer you to a local nonprofit that helps refugees. They have caseworkers who can help you with this. The name of the organization is World Refugee Assistance, and their number is 709-555-1525.

Client: [refuses to accept this suggestion]

Before acting out the role play, write down good arguments/points that the interpreter could make to convince the client to go to the other agency. Then, for the rest of the role play, use spontaneous discussion.

_____
_____
_____
_____

Note: The client should resist the interpreter's suggestion. Make it tough for the interpreter to say no! But the interpreter should remain calm, professional and warm.

Exercise 5-e   Reviewing Standards

In small groups, review the NCIHC National Standards of Practice. Identify:

- The standard of practice that your group finds the most *surprising* (or would have considered most surprising before taking this training).
- The standard of practice that your group expects will be the most *difficult* or challenging to adhere to in real life after this training ends.

_____
_____
_____

Exercise 5-f   Standards Role Play Game

Your instructor will select one of the two following activities:

1) The instructor will distribute one slip of paper to each group. Each slip of paper will contain one of the ten challenges to respecting standards that are listed in pp. 337-348 of your manual. Your small group will create a role play acting out the situation represented by that challenge. When it is time to act out the role play, the rest of the class will have to guess which challenge (e.g. Challenge #4) your group's role play represents and the corresponding standards of practice involved.

2) Pick one of the 32 NCIHC Standards of Practice and develop a role play to act out how that standard is being violated. When it is time to act out the role play in front of the class, the rest of the class will have to guess which standard of practice your group is acting out.

Exercise 5-g   Setting Boundaries: Role Plays

Following the directions of the instructor, execute one or all of the role plays below.

TEXT A   HEALTHCARE: Community Health Center

Number of Participants: 2
Roles: Nurse, interpreter
Setting: CHC prenatal clinic

Nurse: Gosh, is she pregnant *again?*
Interpreter: (interprets, then turns to the nurse) Excuse me, as the interpreter I'd like to remind you that I have to interpret everything that is said. (Interprets this to the patient)

Alternative script

Nurse: Gosh, is she pregnant *again?*
Interpreter: (does not interpret, then turns to the nurse) Excuse me, as the interpreter I would like to remind you that I have to interpret everything that is said, and what you just said might be very offensive if I interpret it.

Interpreter: (to patient, in target language) Excuse me, as the interpreter I informed the nurse that something she said was very difficult for me to interpret in a nice [good/polite] way and reminded her that I'm obligated to interpret everything.

Note: The normal protocol is to interpret <u>everything</u>, *particularly if the provider intends those words to be interpreted. Some specialists in the profession feel that in the case of (a) providers who are genuinely not trying to be offensive (or are not even aware of their insensitivity) and (b) are speaking only to the interpreter and don't really understand that the interpreter must interpret what was said, the interpreter may offer the provider one opportunity to rephrase. However, there is no national consensus on this issue. Remember.* <u>**When in doubt—interpret**</u>.

TEXT B   EDUCATION: Parent-Teacher Conference

Number of Participants: 4
Roles: Teacher, parent, teenager, teacher's assistant/interpreter
Setting: High school classroom

Teacher: Mr. Singh, I'm so glad you've come here today.

Father: I'm very upset with my son's grades. Why is he doing so poorly? He used to have fantastic grades.

Teacher: I understand that, and I'm sorry he's having some difficulty.

Teenage son: Dad, calm down, it's not that important.

> The father suddenly explodes: he begins shouting at his son over the boy's poor grades, his laziness and attitude. They trade insults, yelling and cursing. The anxious teacher tells the bilingual employee (who is also the teacher's assistant in the classroom), "Can't you do something?" The interpreter continues to interpret, simultaneously if possible, but does not interrupt the two speakers. The father and son storm out to fight in the hallway. Then the interpreter explains to the teacher that when she is acting as the interpreter she cannot also be the teacher's assistant and must restrict her role to interpreting.

TEXT C   HUMAN AND SOCIAL SERVICES: Conflict of interest

Number of Participants: 3
Roles: Income support specialist, male customer, interpreter
Setting: Social services office

The interpreter is asked to interpret for a man she recognizes as the young man who is dating and abusing her cousin. She respectfully declines to interpret, stating a conflict of interest because she knows the man.

When he and social worker insist they are happy to let her stay to interpret anyway, the interpreter quietly insists this is not appropriate. The man leaves. Afterwards, the interpreter discloses the reason to the provider behind the conflict of interest.

Activity 5-h　　　　　　　**Professional Development**

Identify those standards of practice that are your weakest areas (write down the numbers, e.g., #1, #16, #32).

_____
_____
_____

Working in pairs, list any activities that will help you continue your professional development and strengthen your weakest areas after you complete this program.

_____
_____
_____
_____
_____
_____
_____
_____

After the class has discussed strategies for professional development, write down anything you heard that is not on the list above and that you would like to do yourself.

_____
_____
_____
_____
_____
_____
_____
_____

Now pick the three activities from the two lists above that you intend to focus on most during the next six months to help you improve your interpreting.

_____
_____
_____

Regardless of cost or convenience (you may wave a magic wand) what is the single strategy for professional development you like best and would love to do first if there were no practical obstacles?

_____
_____

SUPPLEMENTARY ROLE PLAYS

NOTE: The following role plays may be used to supplement the program, at the instructor's discretion. Some of these role plays include scripts for Spanish, and some do not.

Role plays <u>without</u> Spanish scripts provide opportunities for Spanish interpreters to practice their sight translation skills (when they play the role of client and sight translate that text into the target language).

These supplementary role plays are also intended to provide extra work for groups who perform role plays more quickly than other groups and/or those groups that may need extra, challenging or sector-specific role plays.

ROLE PLAYS IN HEALTHCARE SETTINGS

HEALTHCARE: Urgent Care

Triage nurse: Hello, how can I help you?

Patient: Necesito ver al doctor. Me caí de mi bicicleta y me he lastimado mi pierna.

Triage nurse: Tell me what happened, when did you fall?

Patient: Hace como media hora. Me caí de mi motocicleta; un idiota se me metió en la glorieta en el Jolly Miller. No iba rápido pero el camino estaba mojado, y cuando el otro chofer me obligó a dar vuelta rápidamente, la moto patinó y me caí. No me importaría pero no había más tráfico. No había necesidad de hacer eso, él simplemenete no estaba poniendo atención. Qué bueno que tenía mi casco puesto. Pero mire la condición de mis jeans—¡estaban nuevos!

Triage nurse: Well, let's have a look. Does your knee hurt? That's a nasty graze you've got there, and it'll be an impressive bruise.

Patient: La rodilla no me duele mucho, pero el tobillo y la muñeca sí. Y la cara se me agarró con algo cuando cayó la moto.

Triage nurse: Yes, that'll need a couple of stitches, but it shouldn't leave a bad scar. We need to get your boot off and look at this ankle. Do you want to take it off yourself, or shall I do it? It'll probably hurt less if you do it.

Triage nurse: Hello, how can I help you?

Patient: I need to see a doctor. I fell off my bike and hurt my leg.

Triage nurse: Tell me what happened, when did you fall?

Patient: About half an hour ago. I fell off my motorcycle. Some idiot got me at the intersection of Jolly Miller. He wasn't going fast, but the road was wet, and when the other driver forced me to turn quickly, the bike slid and I fell. It wouldn't have upset me but there was no other traffic. He didn't need to do it, he simply wasn't paying attention. Good thing I had my helmet on! But look at the state my jeans are in—and they were new!

Triage nurse: Well, let's have a look. Does your knee hurt? That's a nasty graze you've got there, and it'll be an impressive bruise.

Patient: My knee doesn't hurt much, but my ankle and wrist do. And my face made contact with something when the bike fell.

Triage nurse: Yes, that'll need a couple of stitches, but it shouldn't leave a bad scar. We need to get your boot off and look at this ankle. Do you want to take it off yourself, or shall I do it? It'll probably hurt less if you do it.

Patient: Voy a tratar de quitármela. Me duele mucho el talón. Se ve muy hinchado—¿cree que está roto?

Triage nurse: I don't know till I can look at it properly. Let me see—can you move your toes? OK. Now, I'll tell you what's going to happen next. We'll get you down to X-ray, and while we're waiting for a slot there, we can fill your forms in and get that cut on your face seen to. You did say you were wearing a helmet, didn't you? So the other thing is that the police would like to talk to you later on, because there may be an issue of dangerous driving, but that will have to wait until we're sure you're fit to be interviewed. However, your sister has arrived and, if you want, I'll show her in here and she can wait with you. Is that all right? The interpreter will be nearby if you need to ask for anything. So I'll just call your sister and then I'll go and arrange for the X-rays. A member of staff will come and stitch that cut, and then the porter will be along to fetch you. It'll be fine for your sister to come with you to radiography if you want her to, but she won't be able to come inside with you. Of course, the interpreter will have to go back with you—but they're used to that. OK? So I'll be back in a tick.

Patient: I'll try to take it off. My heel hurts a lot. It looks very swollen—do you think it's broken?

Triage nurse: I don't know till I can look at it properly. Let me see—can you move your toes? OK. Now, I'll tell you what's going to happen next. We'll get you down to X-ray, and while we're waiting for a slot there, we can fill your forms in and get that cut on your face seen to. You did say you were wearing a helmet, didn't you? So the other thing is that the police would like to talk to you later on, because there may be an issue of dangerous driving, but that will have to wait until we're sure you're fit to be interviewed. However, your sister has arrived and, if you want, I'll show her in here and she can wait with you. Is that all right? The interpreter will be nearby if you need to ask for anything. So I'll just call your sister and then I'll go and arrange for the X-rays. A member of staff will come and stitch that cut, and then the porter will be along to fetch you. It'll be fine for your sister to come with you to radiography if you want her to, but she won't be able to come inside with you. Of course, the interpreter will have to go back with you—but they're used to that. OK? So I'll be back in a tick.

HEALTHCARE: Retinoblastoma

Doctor: Mr. Abad, after carefully reviewing all the tests done on your son, we are sure that your son has **retinoblastoma.**

Parent: ¿Puede explicarme eso? ¿Qué es eso?

Doctor: Retinoblastoma is a disease of the eye.

Parent: Qué tipo de enfermedad?

Doctor: Cells have multiplied quickly in your son's eye, forming a tumor in the retina.

Parent: ¿¡Un tumor?! Estoy seguro que usted puede operar el tumor y liberarlo de ese tumor, ¿verdad?

Doctor: Well it is not that easy, the tumor has filled his eyeball

Parent: ¿Qué está tratando de decirme? ¿No puede operarle el ojo?

Doctor: There are some treatments available.

Parent: Qué bueno, ¿cuándo empezamos?

Doctor: Before I can discuss treatment, I must explain other things. Your son will be losing his sight and will become blind. We do not know how long this will take but we know he will not be able to see. I want you to understand this.

Parent: ¡NO! ¡¡ESTO NO PUEDE SUCEDER!! ¡¡¡NO!!!

Doctor: Mr. Abad, after carefully reviewing all the tests done on your son, we are sure that your son has **retinoblastoma.**

Parent: Can you explain this to me? What is it?

Doctor: Retinoblastoma is a disease of the eye.

Parent: What type of disease?

Doctor: Cells have multiplied quickly in your son's eye, forming a tumor in the retina.

Parent: A tumor?! But I'm sure you can operate on the tumor and get it out, right?

Doctor: Well it is not that easy, the tumor has filled his eyeball

Parent: What are you trying to tell me? You can't operate on his eye?

Doctor: There are some treatments available.

Parent: Great, when do we start?

Doctor: Before I can discuss treatment, I must explain other things. Your son will be losing his sight and will become blind. We do not know how long this will take but we know he will not be able to see. I want you to understand this.

Parent: NO!!! THIS CAN'T BE HAPPENING!! NO!!!

Parent: A el le fascina leer y está aprendiendo a manejar. ¡El quiere ir a la escuela y quiere ir a la universidad! El es un alumno nuevo y tiene muchas ilusiones con su futuro.

Doctor: We will have to refer him to other specialists and make sure he receives special services in school since he is going to go blind. I am going to schedule him for an immediate follow up appointment with Dr. Good so he can discuss treatment with you. I recommend you set up an appointment as soon as possible.

Doctor: Mr. Abad, I received your son's medical file and I have reviewed it carefully. I am very sorry that your son has this disease.

Parent: ¿Es un tumor en su ojo pero usted es el especialista, usted puede operarlo y sacarle esa cosa, cierto?

Doctor: Yes, we can operate but that is not going to resolve the problem since your son will lose his vision. It's completely taken over by these tumors. More in the right eye than on the left eye.

Parent: ¿Pero va a poder ver algo en su ojo derecho, cierto?

Doctor: Maybe for a little while but I do not know how much or for how long.

Parent: ¿Por qué? ¿Qué la cirugía no va a resolver el problema? POR FAVOR, POR FAVOR, SE LO RUEGO, ¡¡¡AYUDE A MI HIJO!!!

Parent: He loves to read and he's learning how to drive. He wants to go to school and he wants to go to college! He's a new student and he has a lot of dreams about his future.

Doctor: We will have to refer him to other specialists and make sure he receives special services in school since he is going to go blind. I am going to schedule him for an immediate follow up appointment with Dr. Good so he can discuss treatment with you. I recommend you set up an appointment as soon as possible.

Doctor: Mr. Abad, I received your son's medical file and I have reviewed it carefully. I am very sorry that your son has this disease.

Parent: It's a tumor in his eye but you're the specialist, you can operate on him and get this thing out for sure, right?

Doctor: Yes, we can operate but that is not going to resolve the problem since your son will lose his vision. It's completely taken over by these tumors. More in the right eye than on the left eye.

Parent: But he'll be able to see with his right eye, right?

Doctor: Maybe for a little while but I do not know how much or for how long.

Parent: Why? Isn't surgery going to take care of the problem? PLEASE, PLEASE, I'M BEGGING YOU, HELP MY CHILD!!!

Doctor: Well, the cells that caused the tumor have spread out of the eye, and they're cancerous cells. I'm afraid your son has cancer.

Parent: ¡¡CANCER!! ¡¡¡CANCER!!! NO ¡¿POR QUE?! ¿¡POR QUE EL?! ¿POR QUE YO? ¡NO!

Doctor: I am very sorry. We'll do the best we can. We don't know how he is going to respond to treatment but we are talking about something very aggressive. Your child will no longer be able to go to school. You might want to make some arrangements since this treatment is going to make him feel very ill.

Doctor: Well, the cells that caused the tumor have spread out of the eye, and they're cancerous cells. I'm afraid your son has cancer.

Parent: CANCER!! CANCER!!! NO!! WHY?! WHY HIM?! ¿WHY ME? NO!

Doctor: I am very sorry. We'll do the best we can. We don't know how he is going to respond to treatment but we are talking about something very aggressive. Your child will no longer be able to go to school. You might want to make some arrangements since this treatment is going to make him feel very ill.

HEALTHCARE: Psychiatric Evaluation

Psychiatrist: Do you feel depressed, sad or burned out?

Patient: Bueno…si. Me siento muy triste, bastante; casi todos los días, especialmente si veo TV en donde salen niños. Imagínese, no voy a llegar a ver crecer a mis hijos!

Psychiatrist: TV shows with children? I want to hear more about it but for now, we need to move on. Have you ever tried to harm yourself?

Patient: No, ¡pero quiero matar ese doctor! ¿Cómo me pudo hacer esto? ¡*Lo odio*!

Psychiatrist: Which doctor are you talking about?

Patient: ¡Aquél ese, el de la clínica! ¡Semejante *idiota*!

Psychiatrist: I understand that you are angry, but I also understand that the misdiagnosis was caused by the lab, not the doctor. Is that correct?

Patient: ¡Que mierda! El también es responsable. El laboratorio revolvió las sangres pero él es responsable; después de todo, ¡él es el doctor!

Psychiatrist: I see, when you say you want to kill the doctor, do you really mean that? Do you have a specific plan?

Patient: Usted también, está lleno de mierda. ¿Qué quiere decir, un plan? ¿¡Matarlo quiere decir matarlo, cierto!? ¿Qué quiere que yo le diga? Hay que barbaridad otro más que es pura mierda….

Psychiatrist: Do you feel depressed, sad or burned out?

Patient: Mmm…yes. I feel very sad, and stressed; almost every day and especially if I watch TV shows where I see children. Can you imagine, I'm not going to be able to see my children grow up?

Psychiatrist: TV shows with children? I want to hear more about it but for now, we need to move on. Have you ever tried to harm yourself?

Patient: No, but I want to kill that doctor! How could he do something like that? *I hate him!*

Psychiatrist: Which doctor are you talking about?

Patient: That one, the one from the clinic! Such an *idiot*!

Psychiatrist: I understand that you are angry, but I also understand that the misdiagnosis was caused by the lab, not the doctor. Is that correct?

Patient: What kind of shit is this! He is responsible. The lab mixed the blood but he is responsible; after all, he is the doctor!

Psychiatrist: I see, when you say you want to kill the doctor, do you really mean that? Do you have a specific plan?

Patient: You too, so full of shit. What do you mean, a plan? Kill is kill, right? What do you want me to tell you? Oh my, another one... so much shit….

HEALTHCARE: Abortion

Counselor: Lety, according to the laws in this state, no one can perform an abortion unless you have parental consent. Where are your parents?

Patient: Bueno no importa, mis padres son buena onda y mi novio va a pagar por esto.

Counselor: I see. And how old is your boyfriend?

Patient: El ya es mayor, ya casi tiene 17 pero tiene un trabajo en el Wendy's y el puede pagar por esto.

Counselor: That's still an issue. I cannot discuss the situation with him and again, I need your parents to discuss this.

Patient: Ya le dije, mi novio y mis padres son buena onda y están de acuerdo con esto. No necesito arruinar mi vida ahora. Esto fue solo un error y mis padres están bien con esto.

Counselor: We need to discuss the risks of this procedure.

Patient: Bien, al grano. ¿Que necesito saber? ¿Un aborto es un aborto, cierto?

Counselor: Well, yes and no. There are some risks involved but before I even start with this, by law, I have to have a parent or their permission for me to discuss this.

Patient: ¡Usted si que la friega! ¿Qué problema tiene? Soy suficientemente mayor. ¡Ya tengo 16 años!

Counselor: Lety, according to the laws in this state, no one can perform an abortion unless you have parental consent. Where are your parents?

Patient: Well, it doesn't matter, they're cool with this and my boyfriend will pay for it.

Counselor: I see. And how old is your boyfriend?

Patient: He is old, he is almost 17 but he has a job at Wendy's and he can pay for it.

Counselor: That's still an issue. I cannot discuss the situation with him and again, I need your parents to discuss this.

Patient: I told you, my boyfriend and my parents are cool with this. I don't need to ruin my life now. This was only a little mistake and my parents are fine with it.

Counselor: We need to discuss the risks of this procedure.

Patient: Good, straight to the point. What do I need to know? An abortion is an abortion, right?

Counselor: Well, yes and no. There are some risks involved but before I even start with this, by law, I have to have a parent or their permission for me to discuss this.

Patient: Man, you really suck! What's your problem? I am old enough, I'm 16 years old!

ROLE PLAYS IN EDUCATIONAL SETTINGS

EDUCATION: Deposition (Legal interpreting)

Attorney General's Office (AGO): Good Morning, Mr. Garcia. I am Allison Landry with the Attorney General's Office, and I represent affected Universities of the Commonwealth of Virginia and their Presidents and Boards of Visitors whom you and EAE have sued in this case.

AGO: Mr. Garcia, have you ever been deposed before? Or involved in any other lawsuits before?

Deponent: No yo nunca me he involucrado o atestiguado en un juicio legal.

AGO: What does EAE stand for?

Deponent: Las siglas indican Acceso Igual a la Educación.

AGO: Who are the founders of EAE?

Deponent: Los que crearon la asociación son los estudiantes, maestros, y ciudadanos.

AGO: Okay, how did the members go about deciding to become an organization?

Deponent: Lo que recuerdo, fueron parte de reuniones que tuvimos con un grupo de líderes estudiantiles y de las preguntas que ellos tenían acerca del ingreso de estudiantes indocumentados a las universidades y del memorándum del Fiscal General del estado de Virginia.

AGO: Okay, now your bylaws say that the purpose of this group is to promote the welfare and education of all minority and immigrant individuals. What kind of minorities are you talking about?

Attorney General's Office (AGO): Good Morning, Mr. Garcia. I am Allison Landry with the Attorney General's Office, and I represent affected Universities of the Commonwealth of Virginia and their Presidents and Boards of Visitors whom you and EAE have sued in this case.

AGO: Mr. Garcia, have you ever been deposed before? Or involved in any other lawsuits before?

Deponent: No, I've never been involved in or testified for a lawsuit.

AGO: What does EAE stand for?

Deponent: The initials stand for Equal Access to Education.

AGO: Who are the founders of EAE?

Deponent: The people who established the association are students, teachers and local citizens.

AGO: Okay, how did the members go about deciding to become an organization?

Deponent: From what I can remember, they were part of meetings we had with a group of student leaders and questions they had about undocumented students entering universities and a memorandum from the Attorney General of Virginia.

AGO: Okay, now your bylaws say that the purpose of this group is to promote the welfare and education of all minority and immigrant individuals. What kind of minorities are you talking about?

Deponent: Todas las minorías pueden ser miembros del asociación.

AGO: It goes on to say that your membership includes current and former students of Virginia public high schools. Is that correct?

Deponent: Si, eso es cierto.

AGO: Okay, well, when you say that one of the purposes is to obtain access for all people, including those with undocumented status, what do you mean by that?

Deponent: Mi interpretación es que sí, queremos acceso educativo para personas que son indocumentadas.

AGO: In the membership of the organization, there are students who are in college and those who are planning to apply to Virginia universities. Do you know the immigration status of the individuals? Are some of them citizens?

Deponent: Si, unos son ciudadanos y otros no.

AGO: Remember green card does not mean citizenship. Are you a U.S. citizen?

Deponent: Si, yo soy cuidadano de los Estados Unidos.

AGO: Do you know that some of your members have been admitted to the universities that your group has sued? And why do you continue to sue these universities?

Deponent: Lo único que puedo decirle es que el proceso de aplicar fue difícil cuando ellos aplicaron y nunca estaban seguros si los habían aceptado y si calificaban para la matricula residentes o no.

Deponent: All minorities can be members of the association.

AGO: It goes on to say that your membership includes current and former students of Virginia public high schools. Is that correct?

Deponent: Yes, that's quite true.

AGO: Okay, well, when you say that one of the purposes is to obtain access for all people, including those with undocumented status, what do you mean by that?

Deponent: My interpretation is that yes, we want equal access to education for people who are undocumented.

AGO: In the membership of the organization, there are students who are in college and those who are planning to apply to Virginia universities. Do you know the immigration status of the individuals? Are some of them citizens?

Deponent: Yes, some of them are citizens and others aren't.

AGO: Remember green card does not mean citizenship. Are you a U.S.citizen?

Deponent: Yes, I am a citizen of the United States.

AGO: Do you know that some of your members have been admitted to the universities that your group has sued? And why do you continue to sue these universities?

Deponent: All I can tell you is that the process of applying was very difficult for them and they were never sure if they were accepted and if they qualified for in-state registration or not.

Registration Intake Center

Parent: Buenos días.

Provider: Good morning

Parent: Recién llegamos a este país y necesito matricular a mi hija.

Provider: You need to call the Intake Center for an appointment at 703-555-1212, between 7:30 a.m. and 4:00 p.m.

Parent: Pero yo salgo de trabajar a las 5:00 p.m. y no tengo tiempo antes.

Provider: I'm sorry, but you will have to call them during that time.

Parent: Está bien.

Provider: The day of the appointment, the student should come to the Intake Center with a parent or legal guardian.

Parent: Mi comadre va a venir porque yo voy a trabajar.

Provider: Is she the legal guardian?

Parent: No, pero yo le doy permiso para que haga todas esas cosas. Ella es bien buena y me ayuda cuando sabe que tengo necesidad.

Provider: I'm sorry but if she is not the legal guardian you need to come.

Parent: Está bien. ¿Y la dirección?

Parent: Good morning.

Provider: Good morning

Parent: We have just come to this country and I need to register my daughter.

Provider: You need to call the Intake Center for an appointment at 703-555-1212, between 7:30 a.m. and 4:00 p.m.

Parent: But I get off of work at 5:00 p.m. and don't have time before then.

Provider: I'm sorry, but you will have to call them during that time.

Parent: All right.

Provider: The day of the appointment, the student should come to the Intake Center with a parent or legal guardian.

Parent: My friend will come because I go to work.

Provider: Is she the legal guardian?

Parent: No, but I give her permission to do all of these kinds of things. She is very nice and helps me out when she knows I need her.

Provider: I'm sorry but if she is not the legal guardian you need to come.

Parent: OK. What is the address?

Provider: The address is: Intake Center, Clarendon Education Center, 2801 Clarendon Blvd., Suite #305, Arlington, VA 22201.

Parent: ¿Y eso queda lejos?

Provider: I don't know where you're coming from.

Parent: Si es por Clarendon, ha de ser por los shopping, ¿verdad?

Provider: Yes, there are restaurants and shops near there. It's in walking distance from the Clarendon Metro Station. Please, plan to stay for one hour or more at the Intake Center.

Parent: ¿Y por qué tanto tiempo? Yo no puedo perder mucho en mi trabajo, me pueden botar. El otro día, botaron a un chavo solo por que se atrasó unos minutos. La Niña Carmen dijo que quizás no tenía necesidad.

Provider: The registration appointment takes at least an hour. They make an evaluation of the student's academic record. They give tests to the student to determine their knowledge of English and level of reading and writing skills in his or her native language, if they can. The student will also be tested for mathematics skills. That assessment process may take from 20-30 minutes for kindergarteners or preschoolers, up to several hours for middle and high school students.

Provider: The address is: Intake Center, Clarendon Education Center, 2801 Clarendon Blvd., Suite #305, Arlington, VA 22201.

Parent: Is that far?

Provider: I don't know where you're coming from.

Parent: If it's by Clarendon, it must be by the shopping center, right?

Provider: Yes, there are restaurants and shops near there. It's in walking distance from the Clarendon Metro Station. Please, plan to stay for one hour or more at the Intake Center.

Parent: Why so much time? I can't miss much work, they might fire me. The other day, they fired a guy just because he was a few minutes late. Carmen said maybe he didn't really need the job.

Provider: The registration appointment takes at least an hour. They make an evaluation of the student's academic record. They give tests to the student to determine their knowledge of English and level of reading and writing skills in his or her native language, if they can. The student will also be tested for mathematics skills. That assessment process may take from 20-30 minutes for kindergarteners or preschoolers, up to several hours for middle and high school students.

Parent: Mi hija no sabe inglés, ni escribir. Es bien huraña, la van a poner nerviosa. Fíjese que la profe me dijo que tenía problemas con la emoción y necesita un psicólogo.

Provider: Yes, I understand. That is why it is very important for her to be tested. The exams will help us place her in the right class.

Parent: Yo le digo esto porque también es sorda y a mí me cuesta a veces que ponga atención. Es bien necia. Allá es el pedregueo donde vivíamos en mi pueblo…se lo iba a jugar a la escuela. La profe era bien buena y le tenía pena.

Provider: Don't worry; we'll try to help her as much as we can. Once the registration and assessment processes are complete, the Intake Center staff will give the student and parent an overview of school regulations, attendance, transportation, school calendar, etc. As a final step, the student and parent or guardian will take the registration and assessment documents to the school for student admission.

Parent: ¿Y que no es aquí la escuela?

Provider: No, the school will be in her neighborhood.

Parent: Yo pensé que era aquí. A mí me gusta por las tiendas también para hacer los mandados. ¿Aquí cerca está la tiendona, va?

Parent: My daughter doesn't know English, or how to write. She is very shy; they're going to make her nervous. You know, her teacher told me that she has emotional problems and needs a psychologist.

Provider: Yes, I understand. That is why it is very important for her to be tested. The exams will help us place her in the right class.

Parent: I'm telling you this because she's also deaf, and sometimes it's even hard for me to get her to pay attention. She's very stubborn. We used to live in a town out in the country… she just went to school to play. Her teacher was very nice and felt sorry for her.

Provider: Don't worry; we'll try to help her as much as we can. Once the registration and assessment processes are complete, the Intake Center staff will give the student and parent an overview of school regulations, attendance, transportation, school calendar, etc. As a final step, the student and parent or guardian will take the registration and assessment documents to the school for student admission.

Parent: Isn't the school here?

Provider: No, the school will be in her neighborhood.

Parent: Oh, I thought it was here. I also like it here because of the stores, for doing errands. The wholesale store is near here, isn't it?

Provider: Maybe, I don't know. Now here's a list of documents we need for registration: proof of age and legal name, original birth certificate—

Parent: Fíjese que yo me vine mojada y no tengo esos papeles. Allá yo creo que tal vez me los pueden conseguir pero se va a tardar mucho.

Provider: If you do don't have an original birth certificate, you can bring a passport, I-94 or any other official document that would prove the student's date of birth. However, if you do not have an original birth certificate, you need to fill out and notarize an affidavit they'll give you at the Intake Center stating the reasons why you don't have an original birth certificate. Now, you need to be aware that the student may only be registered if the parent or legal custodian also lives here in Arlington.

Parent: Y que puedo traer para probar que vivo en Arlington?

Provider: You could bring a Rental Agreement/Lease, a Property Title or a notarized statement—you could get a form for that at the Intake Center to prove that the student lives in Arlington County.

Parent: Nosotros le estamos rentando a Don Moncho y yo no sé si va a querer prestarnos esos papeles. Dice que la otra vez, migración lo estaba buscando y se cambió de dirección. Tiene miedo que lo manda de regreso. Es bien desconfiado con uno.

Provider: Maybe, I don't know. Now here's a list of documents we need for registration: proof of age and legal name, original birth certificate—

Parent: The thing is that I came undocumented, and don't have those papers. Back home I think maybe they could get them for me, but it's going to take a long time.

Provider: If you do don't have an original birth certificate, you can bring a passport, I-94 or any other official document that would prove the student's date of birth. However, if you do not have an original birth certificate, you need to fill out and notarize an affidavit they'll give you at the Intake Center stating the reasons why you don't have an original birth certificate. Now, you need to be aware that the student may only be registered if the parent or legal custodian also lives here in Arlington.

Parent: What can I bring to prove that I live in Arlington?

Provider: You could bring a Rental Agreement/Lease, a Property Title or a notarized statement—you could get a form for that at the Intake Center to prove that the student lives in Arlington County.

Parent: We're renting from Don Moncho, and I don't know if he's going to want to give us those papers. He said that one time, immigration was looking for him, so he moved. He's afraid they will send him back. He's very suspicious of people.

120

Provider: Tell him that this is very important for your daughter to go to school and that he doesn't need to worry about immigration. You also need immunization records for your daughter: polio, measles, mumps, rubella, tetanus, diphtheria, whooping cough, influenza, hepatitis, chicken pox, and meningococcal vaccinations. A TB test given within the past year is also mandatory. And for elementary and middle school students you have to bring proof of a physical exam given within the past year.

Parent: Dios mío, me la van a puyar toda a mija. Que yo me acuerde yo nunca le puse inyecciones. Yo la tuve en la casa. La Comadre Chona me ayudó y dijo que venía bien. No nos dimos cuenta que era sorda hasta los cuatro años. Nosotros le hablábamos y se hacia la don nadie.

Provider: Students aren't allowed to enter Arlington Public Schools unless they have all the required vaccinations, the TB test and, for elementary and middle school students, the physical examination.

Parent: Y yo no sé adónde llevarla. Además no sé cuánto me va a costar.

Provider: If she doesn't have her shots, you can get them free of charge at the Department of Human Services. They're open Tuesday from 3:00 to 7:00 p.m. and Friday: 7:30 to 11:00 a.m. A parent or legal guardian has to accompany the child. She also needs her official school records, if you have them.

Provider: Tell him that this is very important for your daughter to go to school and that he doesn't need to worry about immigration. You also need immunization records for your daughter: polio, measles, mumps, rubella, tetanus, diphtheria, whooping cough, influenza, hepatitis, chicken pox, and meningococcal vaccinations. A TB test given within the past year is also mandatory. And for elementary and middle school students you have to bring proof of a physical exam given within the past year.

Parent: Oh my goodness, they're going to stick my daughter all over. I don't remember ever getting her shots. I kept her at home. My friend, Chona, helped me and said that she was doing fine. We didn't realize that she was deaf until she was four years old. When we spoke to her, she would ignore us.

Provider: Students aren't allowed to enter Arlington Public Schools unless they have all the required vaccinations, the TB test and, for elementary and middle school students, the physical examination

Parent: But I don't know where to take her. And I don't know how much it's going to cost, either.

Provider: If she doesn't have her shots, you can get them free of charge at the Department of Human Services. They're open Tuesday from 3:00 to 7:00 p.m. and Friday: 7:30 to 11:00 a.m. A parent or legal guardian has to accompany the child. She also needs her official school records, if you have them.

EDUCATION: Summer School

Teacher: Your sons have to attend summer school. They have been in the ESL program and they need to come to Summer School so they can move ahead.

Parent: What do you mean? They are not failing right?

Teacher: No, but if they come to summer school, they can move up one more level.

Parent: And why would I want to push them so much, isn't the school teaching them well enough?

Teacher: Yes but the school also wants them to come to summer school so they can continue to learn.

Parent: Well, they help me at work in the summer; they come to work with me. I clean houses and they need to learn to work.

Teacher: But they are only 12 and 13; they do not need to work at this age. And besides, you have to be careful because under the law, they need to be 16 before they go to work.

Parent: In my country, children start working when they are 10 years old so these two are 12 and 13. It is past their time to start working. Besides, we need the extra income and I can't afford summer school. How much is it anyways?

Teacher: Well each class is $100.00 dollars and the classes go for 4 weeks from 9-12 AM.

Parent: Well! $100.00 per class! I have 3 children, how many classes will I have to pay for?

Teacher: At least one for each one let me see... this would be….mmmm.

Parent: Don't even add it up, it's more money than I can afford. I can't do it.

Teacher: Would it be better if we found you financial aid?

Parent: And how much would that be? Remember, I'm a house cleaner. I don't make that much!

Teacher: Yes, I know. How about 50 percent off?

Parent: And how much is that in dollars?

Teacher: Instead of $300.00 you would pay $150.00

Parent: No way, I can't. It's still too much. You have to give it to me free!

EDUCATION: Child with Cystic Fibrosis

Parent: I am not sure whether to share information about my daughter or not. I'm afraid the school will treat her differently.

Counselor: Don't worry. She won't be treated differently. We need to know what her condition is so we can offer more support for her academic success. You submitted some medical records but we would like to hear from you what exactly she needs.

Parent: Well, you know she has cystic fibrosis which is not contagious but she's susceptible to lung infections and she should be isolated from other students when they have flu or something like that. She needs unlimited access to the bathroom since she needs to drink a lot of water.

Counselor: Ok, we can do that. Is there anything else?

Parent: Yes, this is the difficult one. She needs to do airway clearance treatments if necessary. This is very important since if she does not do it, she'll develop respiratory problems.

Counselor: Ok, she can go to the clinic for her treatments. The nurse will need to know how to help her.

Parent: She also needs accommodations for lunch. She has to take enzymes before each snack or meal. Teachers should not allow her to eat anything without her enzymes.

Counselor: Oh, so how would you want to inform the teachers about this? Do you want to have a meeting with all of them at once, or do you prefer to meet with them individually?

Parent: Well, aren't we going to have a 504? This is the part of IDEA that protects her rights, isn't it?

Counselor: Well. Let me clarify. IDEA is the Individuals with Disabilities Education Act and 504 is part of the Rehabilitation Act of 1973. Both of these plans are written agreements between the school and the parents, and you're right, they do outline her needs and accommodations. But it's important we put all this in writing so it's not just a casual conversation. We also need to determine if she needs an IEP. For that, we need to have a meeting. The first one is called Eligibility Meeting. You can request it or we can set it up.

Parent: There's so much paper work! This is very exhausting! Will I always have an interpreter for these meetings?

ROLE PLAYS IN HUMAN AND SOCIAL SERVICE SETTINGS

Sexual Assault Center

Office manager: Good morning. What can I do for you? The receptionist said you wanted to speak to someone in charge.

Mother: Hi. I'm—I'm not sure if this is the right place. And I wanted to speak in a private office, not the waiting room. (Lowers voice.) It's about my daughter. Do you see people who have been... assaulted and hurt?

Office manager: Absolutely. We're the county sexual assault center. What happened to your daughter?

Mother: Well, we had to flee my country because my husband was tortured. And while we were living in the refugee camp—I hate to say this...

Office Manager: Someone hurt your daughter?

Mother: Yes.

Office Manager: How old was she?

Mother: Thirteen. She was raped by two men, and at first she seemed fine. Very brave, but quiet. Since then—we were in the camp about six months and we've been in this country now a year. And suddenly she is so sad and quiet, she can barely study. And she was such a wonderful student! And so cheerful and sweet and kind. And now all she wants to do is sit in her room alone and listen to music. I'm really worried about her. I'm wondering if it was the rapes. But why would it take so long?

Officer Manager: The first thing you need to hear is that this is *not* unusual. In fact, some children who are sexually assaulted don't begin to feel it for many years. So we'd be happy to see her. I think we might really be able to help her.

Mother: But... How would that work, exactly?

Office Manager: First, we'd like to have her come for an intake exam with a therapist to find out what she needs. Then I suspect they'll recommend individual therapy sessions, maybe once a week. I have to warn you there's a waiting list, but sometimes younger clients and more urgent cases move up the list faster. Do you know if your daughter has had any thoughts of hurting herself?

Mother: I don't know, but she says things like she doesn't see the point in going on and life isn't worth very much—human life is too cheap. Things like that.

Office Manager: Well, that concerns me. In that case we'd really like to see her as soon as possible. But I'm going to give you a number to call in case she needs help right away—it's our 24 hour crisis hotline, and it's *completely* anonymous and safe. She can say anything, she doesn't have to give her name. But if she's at any kind of risk, the hotline counselors will know what to do.

Mother: There's something I have to tell you. First, we have no money.

Office Manager: That's no problem. We do sliding scale. I can hook you up with someone who'll help you fill out a form and then you provide proof of income—pay stubs or last year's taxes. But please know we never turn away anyone for financial reasons. So you might end up paying $10 per session or even less. Please don't worry about money.

Mother: The second thing is more difficult. In our culture—well—these things are not discussed. There's so much shame attached to it. And my husband doesn't even know I'm here, or my daughter. Because it would be hard for them to hear what I'm doing today. I only heard about you through a friend whose daughter came here, and you helped her.

Office Manager: We know there are a lot of complicated cultural issues about sexual assault. Not just in your culture—in almost every culture. That's where you can help us, by giving us all the cultural information you can to help us with your daughter. Our therapists are always trying to research the culture too. But everything you can tell us can be important, because it's cultural information about *your* family, and we'll be happy to listen.

Mother: Thank you. I only want to see her happy again. That's all that matters to me.

HUMAN SERVICES: Public Library

Staff member: How can I help you?

Patron: I'm very upset. Look, I just got a threatening letter about a library fine.

Staff member (glances at letter): Yes. This letter is from the collection agency that we use, Unique Management System. I'm sorry but when your overdue items are more than $25 and the overdue bill is 60 days old, we send the bill to a collection agency.

Patron: A collection agency? For a few children's videos? That's ridiculous.

Staff member: I can see you ran up quite a fine there. But did you know you can renew in person, by phone or online? We even have an automated renewal phone line. Or you can just drop the videos off at any library branch, any time—24/7.

Patron: I brought them back a while ago, but they weren't overdue. We just had them for three weeks.

Staff member: Three weeks? But DVDs are loaned out for one week. And the fines are $1.00 per day. That explains it. Would you like to pay now? You can pay by credit card, or here in person at the library with a check or cash. Or by mail. However you prefer.

Patron: A dollar a day! That's not what I was told when I got the card two months ago!

Staff member: If you can't pay the fine all at once, we can set you up on a payment system so you're paying just one part of the fine at a time.

Patron: (turns to the interpreter and tells the interpreter) This lady is a stinking heap of old fish. What does she think, we're rich? They're just out to screw foreigners because they think we're stupid.

Now improvise the rest of the role play and see what the interpreter does.

HUMAN SERVICES: Department of Permitting Services

Clerk: Hi, I'm Amy Winters. Is there something I can help you with?

Customer: Yes, I got this document off the Montgomery County website, but I don't really understand it. (Hands paper to provider)

Clerk: Oh, this just says you'll need a Certificate of Use and Occupancy because you're opening a new business in Montgomery County.

INTERPRETER: (interprets everything except "certificate of use and occupancy," repeating that term in English, then addresses the provider.) Excuse me, as the interpreter I wanted to tell you I am not aware of an exact equivalent for "certificate of use and occupancy" in [Mandarin, Russian, or your working language]. So that I can interpret it accurately, could you please explain this term? (Interpreter then interprets for the client, e.g., *Excuse me, as the interpreter I just told Ms. Winters that I wasn't aware of an exact equivalent for "certificate of occupancy" and asked her to explain that term so I can interpret it accurately for you.*)

Clerk: Sure, I'll be happy to explain. It's nothing to worry about. What the Use and Occupancy certificate means is, well, the purpose of the certificate is to document that the use is permitted, and that you've met all the applicable safety code and health code requirements. So then you'll have to submit the completed Use and Occupancy application with a copy of the site parking analysis. That's basically a plan that shows where your customers will park to get to your business.

HUMAN SERVICES: Transportation ID

Provider: Our officials have decided to issue special identification passes to some students that could restrict their use of subsidized public transportation.

Client: ¿Puede explicar que es el transporte subsidiado?

Provider: Up until now, students could use public transportation for half the cost by using their school ID. But with the increase we're seeing in young people running in groups taking advantage of people, we feel we need to implement a special identification system. The new ID card will identify the students by name and school.

Client: No creo que esto funcione, los alumnos pueden perder o intercambiar su identificación.

Provider: The new system will have a chip in the ID and can restrict travel after 8 PM.

Client: ¿Entonces, esto quiere decir que mi hija no puede ir a trabajar después de las 8:00? Ella sale de trabajar a las 9:30 PM. ¿Que se supone que hagamos? ¿Sugiere algo?

Provider: The problem is that our city has become unsafe because of the number of youth stealing phones and devices from bus and metro riders.

Provider: Our officials have decided to issue special identification passes to some students that could restrict their use of subsidized public transportation.

Client: Can you please explain what subsidized transportation is?

Provider: Up until now, students could use public transportation for half the cost by using their school ID. But with the increase we're seeing in young people running in groups taking advantage of people, we feel we need to implement a special identification system. The new ID card will identify the students by name and school.

Client: I don't think this will work; students can lose or trade their ID.

Provider: The new system will have a chip in the ID and can restrict travel after 8 PM.

Client: So this means that my daughter can't go to work after 8 PM? She gets off at 9:30 PM. What are we supposed to do? Do you have suggestions?

Provider: The problem is that our city has become unsafe because of the number of youth stealing phones and devices from bus and metro riders.

Client: No todos los jóvenes están metidos en esas cosas, ¿por qué castigar a los chicos trabajadores?

Provider: Remember that the city has curfew for anyone under 17 years old and it's different depending on the time of the year and day.

Client: Lo sé pero dependemos del sueldo de mi hija para salir adelante. ¿Qué podemos hacer?

Provider: There are some options. If your daughter works that late, it means she is older than 17 so the ID won't allow her to use subsidized travel but she can pay full price and still travel. You can also make arrangements to pick her up.

Client: Este plan no me gusta, pero puede que ayude a tener una ciudad más segura.

Client: Not all youth are involved in these things. Why punish the hard-working ones?

Provider: Remember that the city has curfew for anyone under 17 years old and it's different depending on the time of the year and day.

Client: I know but we rely on my daughter's help to get by. What can we do?

Provider: There are some options. If your daughter works that late, it means she is older than 17 so the ID won't allow her to use subsidized travel but she can pay full price and still travel. You can also make arrangements to pick her up.

Client: I don't like this plan, but it might help keep the city safer.

HUMAN SERVICES: SNAP (Food Stamps)

Customer[2]: ¿Cómo puedo conseguir estampillas de comida? [3]

Customer: How can I get food stamps?

Income support specialist (ISS): Anyone can apply for supplemental nutrition assistance. To get it, you and the other people in your household have to meet certain conditions.

Income support specialist (ISS): Anyone can apply for supplemental nutrition assistance. To get it, you and the other people in your household have to meet certain conditions.

Customer: ¿Puede decirme cuáles son estas condiciones?

Customer: Can you tell me what the conditions are?

ISS: Everyone applying in your household must either have or apply for a Social Security number and be a U.S. citizen, U.S. national or have status as a qualified alien. Generally, your household can't have more than $2,000 in resources. But, if your household includes a person age 60 or older or who is disabled, the limit is $3,000.

ISS: Everyone applying in your household must either have or apply for a Social Security number and be a U.S. citizen, U.S. national or have status as a qualified alien. Generally, your household can't have more than $2,000 in resources. But, if your household includes a person age 60 or older or who is disabled, the limit is $3,000.

Customer: ¿Qué quiere decir eso?

Customer: What does that mean?

ISS: These are just the requirements. Oh, and if anyone in your household gets Supplemental Security Income (SSI) or benefits under the Temporary Assistance for Needy Families (TANF) program, that's okay—we don't count that income for this program. So when we say resources, what we mean is cash,

ISS: These are just the requirements. Oh, and if anyone in your household gets Supplemental Security Income (SSI) or benefits under the Temporary Assistance for Needy Families (TANF) program, that's okay—we don't count that income for this program. So when we say resources, what we mean is cash,

---

[2] Most Departments of Social Services refer to clients as "customers."

[3] Departments of Social Services officially no longer use the term "food stamps." The name of the program is SNAP (Supplemental Nutrition Assistance Program). Colloquially, however, most clients and many providers still talk about food stamps.

bank accounts and any savings you have anywhere else.

Customer: Yo no entiendo eso del SSI o el TANF. Yo no tengo papeles pero mi hijo nació en los Estados Unidos. ¿Puedo conseguir estampillas de comida para él?

ISS: Are you a Refugee admitted under section 207 of the Immigration and Nationality Act (INA)?

Customer: Mi marido, sí, pero no ha recibido sus documentos todavía. Mi bebe tiene 2 meses y necesita comida.

ISS: Well, in that case he needs WIC.

Customer: ¿WIC?

ISS: Yes, Women, Infants and Children program. It's a separate program. It gives you supplemental foods, health care referrals, and nutrition education. WIC is for low-income pregnant, breastfeeding or non-breastfeeding women who've given birth, and infants and children up to age five.

bank accounts and any savings you have anywhere else.

Customer: I don't understand SSI or TANF. I am undocumented but my child was born in the USA. Can I get food stamps for him?

ISS: Are you a Refugee admitted under section 207 of the Immigration and Nationality Act (INA)?

Customer: My husband is, but he hasn't received his documents yet. My baby is only 2 months old and he needs food.

ISS: Well, in that case he needs WIC.

Customer: WIC?

ISS: Yes, Women, Infants and Children program. It's a separate program. It gives you supplemental foods, health care referrals, and nutrition education. WIC is for low-income pregnant, breastfeeding or non-breastfeeding women who've given birth, and infants and children up to age five.